ISBN 978-1-5280-1918-7
PIBN 10904382

This book is a reproduction of an important historical work. Forgotten Books uses state-of-the-art technology to digitally reconstruct the work, preserving the original format whilst repairing imperfections present in the aged copy. In rare cases, an imperfection in the original, such as a blemish or missing page, may be replicated in our edition. We do, however, repair the vast majority of imperfections successfully; any imperfections that remain are intentionally left to preserve the state of such historical works.

1 MONTH OF
FREE
READING

at

www.ForgottenBooks.com

By purchasing this book you are eligible for one month membership to ForgottenBooks.com, giving you unlimited access to our entire collection of over 1,000,000 titles via our web site and mobile apps.

To claim your free month visit:

www.forgottenbooks.com/free904382

English
Français
Deutsche
Italiano
Español
Português

www.forgottenbooks.com

Mythology Photography **Fiction**
Fishing Christianity **Art** Cooking
Essays Buddhism Freemasonry
Medicine **Biology** Music **Ancient**
Egypt Evolution Carpentry Physics
Dance Geology **Mathematics** Fitness
Shakespeare **Folklore** Yoga Marketing
Confidence Immortality Biographies
Poetry **Psychology** Witchcraft
Electronics Chemistry History **Law**
Accounting **Philosophy** Anthropology
Alchemy Drama Quantum Mechanics
Atheism Sexual Health **Ancient History**
Entrepreneurship Languages Sport
Paleontology Needlework Islam
Metaphysics Investment Archaeology
Parenting Statistics Criminology
Motivational

Historic, archived document

Do not assume content reflects current
scientific knowledge, policies, or practices.

Augusta, Ga.

CRIMSON CLOVER

HAIRY VETCH.

AUGUSTA EARLY TRUCKER.

CABBAGE SEED
TURNIP SEED
ONION SETS
AND OTHER VEGETABLE SEEDS.
FLOWER SEEDS
AND BULBS.

IMPROVED
AIR

Directions How to Order and Remit.

Write your Name, Post Office, County and State on every order or letter to us. *Send cash* with order. Observe cost of Postage and include with your remittance. Remit by Post Office or Express Money Order, Drafts on Augusta or New York, or Register your letter. We accept clean Postage Stamps—*not revenue stamps*—same as cash.

NOTE.—*Have* all remittances drawn plainly *Alexander Seed Co.* When convenient, we consider Express Money Orders cheaper and safer.

C. O. D. ORDERS.—We do not ship goods C. O. D. unless one-half the estimated amount of the bill accompanies the order. From this rule we do not deviate.

SHIPPING.—We can mail packages of seed weighing up to four pounds. The rate is eight cents per pound. The Express rate is not any more. If your's is an Express office, so notify us, and we will send in that way. Heavier shipments by Express or Freight, as you direct. Parties ordering shipments by Express or Freight *collect* are expected to take them promptly when they arrive at their destination. This should be thoroughly understood when ordering.

Scale of Rates for Seed.

BY EXPRESS, PREPAID.

1½ pounds	10 cents	1 pound, 10 ounces	11 cents
1¾ pounds	12 cents	1 pound, 14 ounces	13 cents
2 pounds	14 cents	2 pounds, 2 ounces	15 cents
2¼ pounds	16 cents	2 pounds, 6 ounces	17 cents
2½ pounds	18 cents		

From 2 pounds and 10 ounces, add 14 cents for each 24 ounces up to 5 pounds, as for example:

2 pounds and 10 ounces	15 cents.
5 pounds	34 cents.

We also have a special Express rate on seeds which average 35 per cent. less than regular merchandise rate. We suggest that you include in your remittance for small seeds enough to prepay same.

Discounts from Retail Prices on Orders.

Please bear in mind that allowances named below APPLY ONLY TO ORDERS FOR VEGETABLE SEEDS *in packets, ounces, quarter, half and pound packages, pints and quarts at retail prices,* AND NOT ON FIELD SEEDS, CLOVERS AND GRASSES.

Purchaser *remitting Fifty Cents* can order seeds as above *amounting to Sixty Cents.* Purchaser *remitting $1.00* can order seeds as above *amounting to $1.25.* Purchaser *remitting $2.00* can order seeds as above *amounting to $2.50* Purchaser *remitting $3.00* can order seeds as above *amounting to $3 75.* Purchaser *remitting $4 00* can order seeds as above *amounting to $5.00.* Purchaser *remitting $5.00* can order seeds as above *amounting to $6 25.* Purchaser *remitting $7.50* can order seeds as above *amounting to $9 50.* Purchaser *remitting $10.00* can order seeds as above *amounting to $13.00.*

☞All orders must be accompanied with a remittance to receive our liberal discounts.

Seeds for Market Gardeners.

We are in position to give Market or Truck Gardeners as low prices as those of any reputable seed house. Our stocks are the very best to be obtained, true to name and tested. We invite inquiries, and will give prices to those who will write to us. In writing, kindly mention variety, with amount of each article desired.

Seeds for Merchants.

Merchants will find our regular line of papered seeds, which are put up in 2½ cent, 5 cent and 10 cent packets, an attractive packet to sell. Our papers contain as much seed as those of some houses whose price is higher. Our seeds are easy to sell, because they are well known. The wide reputation we have for selling the very highest and best quality of seeds, will be found fully sustained in our papered seeds. Merchants' sales would be largely increased by selling our seeds. We furnish lithograph hangers, almanacs and other literature. *Write for our Wholesale Price List;* also price on any seeds in bulk you need.

We take pleasure in recommending *THE FRUITLAND NURSERIES, of Augusta, Ga.,* established in 1857 by P. J. BERCKMANS, and still conducted by him and his sons, now incorporated as the P. J. BERCKMANS CO. Those wanting *Fruit and Ornamental Trees* suited to our Southern climate cannot be better suited than by dealing with them. Their illustrated Catalogue mailed free by addressing them. Mention our Catalogue.

Alexander Seed Co.

Give no warranty, expressed or implied. While we exercise every effort to procure the best varieties of seeds, and such as are fresh and genuine, we will not be in any way responsible for the crop. Our guarantee does not extend beyond our honest efforts and intentions. If purchaser does not accept the goods on these terms, they must be returned at once.

NOTE.—Further, that all our seeds are tested for germination by an apparatus that has the approval of the United States Department of Agriculture.

In writing, ordering or making out Post Office or Express Money Orders, Checks or Drafts, address plainly,

ALEXANDER SEED CO.,
AUGUSTA, GEORGIA.

Richards & Shaver, Printers, Augusta, Ga.

JULY, 1900.

Summer and Fall Catalogue.

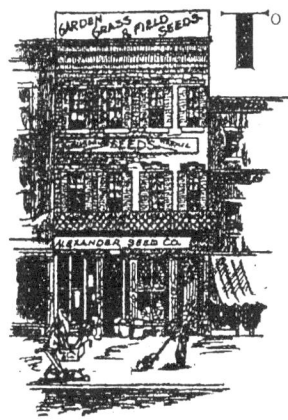

TO OUR FRIENDS AND PATRONS.—It is with appreciation that we take this opportunity to again thank our patrons for their liberal patrouage during the past season, and hundreds of them continuously for so many years. Especially gratifying is it to us that during the past years our orders came so numerously from new customers—those who had not dealt with us before—our last Spring business largely exceeding in bulk and amount that done by us in any previous year. While we naturally attribute this to the known high quality of seeds that we sell, we believe our patrons, who have become acquainted with our methods of doing business and our aim at all times to furnish only such Garden, Grass, Field and Flower Seeds as are best adapted to our Southern soil and climate, appreciate the fact that an order intrusted to us will at all times receive our careful, painstaking efforts to serve them faithfully and well. We have again found it necessary to enlarge our already commodious quarters, and have added another warehouse to our storing capacity, enabling us to carry larger bulk and complete assortment of seeds. Our system of *testing seeds* for germinating quality has the approval of the department at Washington. We carefully test all seeds before sending them out. No honest seedsman would knowingly send out seeds of poor quality; we consider this a crime. Those who deal with us can depend upon our selection of Seeds, Bulbs, Roots, Onion Sets, and every item we sell, as being of the highest quality obtainable. We urge our patrons to send in their orders early;—don't wait until planting time. It is our rule, as near as we can do so, to ship all orders on the day they are received. We call attention to 'Directions for Ordering" on the preceding page. Kindly follow them carefully; in so doing you will save us much time, as well as lessen the possibility of any errors of address or of filling your orders.

Soliciting your continued patronage, we are

Very truly,

ALEXANDER SEED CO.,

Augusta, Georgia.

CONDENSED INDEX.

Good Gardens Made Better by Planting Our Seeds.

In the following pages we list only the *best standard varieties* of *Vegetable Seeds, Grass Seeds, Flower Seeds,* and such other articles as we think will be of value to our patrons.

SEEDS IN PAPERS BY MAIL POSTPAID.

We pay postage on all packets, ounces and one-fourth pounds. *For half pounds add 5 cents; one pound 10 cents; for half pint Peas and Beans add 5 cents; for one pint add 10 cents; for one quart add 15 cents for postage.*

Extra Order Sheets and Envelopes will be mailed free to customers requesting them.

ASPARAGUS ROOTS.

These we furnish in the Fall months.

We can furnish the Palmetto, 100 roots, enough to set a bed 10x40 feet. Good strong two-year-old roots. Price, per 100, 75 cents; 500, $3; 1,000, $5. Write for prices in large quantities.

BEANS FOR LATE CROP.

We advise planting at intervals of two or three weeks from June till September, for succession of Summer crops. You will have abundant yield till killed by frost. Do not plant more than two inches deep, in 18-inch rows, three inches apart in the drill. One quart will plant 100-feet drill. These varieties do best for Summer planting.

Bush Snap Beans.

Again *Bush Beans* are very scarce, therefore so high. Genuine Extra Early Valentine can only be had from a few, and our stock, and the general stock all over the country, of the kinds below named, are very short. For this reason, we would advise those wishing *Bush Beans* to order early.

NEW EXTRA EARLY REFUGEE BEAN.
10 DAYS EARLIER THAN THE "OLD" REFUGEE.

Green Podded Bunch.

New Extra Early Refugee—This Bean has become very popular with the truck farmer. An immense yielder; sure to produce a crop in dry or wet season. It is ready for market ten days earlier than the old Refugee. A fine shipper. It is becoming one of the most popular green podded snaps, both for Spring and Summer. Packet, 5 cents; ½ pint, 15 cents; pint, 20 cents; quart, 35 cents.

Extra Early Improved Valentine—One of the best and earliest. Very productive. We warn our customers against the inferior quality of Valentine that is being offered by some. Price, papers, 2 for 5 cents; ½ pint, 15 cents; pint, 25 cents; quart, 40 cents.

"Best of All"—Very popular; green podded snap and good shell bean. Papers, 2 for 5 cents; ½ pint, 10 cents; pint, 20 cents; quart, 30 cents.

Early Mohawk—Very early and productive. Long, green podded, flat. Papers, 2 for 5 cents; ½ pint, 10 cents; pint, 15 cents; quart, 25 cents.

Alexander Stringless Green Pod—The only stringless green podded bean in cultivation. Pods very wide, thick and fleshy, surpassing all others in crisp, tender flavor. Earlier by two weeks than the Valentine. Sure to prove of great value to the market gardener, as well as for home gardeners. Packet, 10 cents, 3 for 25 cents; pint. 25 cents.

Wax Podded.

Wardwell's Kidney Wax—Very productive, and one of the most popular early wax varieties. A great favorite for shipping; also with the home market and family garden. Pods are tender and long. Packet, 5 cents; ½ pint, 15 cents; pint, 25 cents; quart, 40 cents.

Alexander's Valentine Wax Beans—A comparatively new variety of much merit. Pods, golden wax, foliage large and strong, makes a fine snap. Try it. Packet, 10 cents, 3 for 25 cents; half pint, 15 cents; pint, 25 cents; quart, 40 cents.

Dwarf Black Wax—Very early and delicious; round, yellow pods. Papers, 2 for 5 cents; ½ pint, 15 cents; pint, 20 cents; quart, 35 cents.

BEANS—Wax Podded- Continued.

Mr S. B. Kennerly, Tyler County, Texas, April 5th, 1900, says: "Gentlemen—In 1898 you sent me a complimentary package of Bunch Beans (Scarlet Market Garden Wax), guaranteed to make in thirty-five days from germination. I planted the Beans on the 8th day of August and began eating them on the 14th of September."

BEANS—Wax Podded—Continued.

Dwarf Golden Wax—Very early; round golden pods. Papers, 2 for 5 cents; ½ pint, 10 cents; pint, 15 cents; quart, 30 cents.

Scarlet Market Garden Wax—A variety that we gave away last year as trial package. Our supply is so short of this variety that we can only offer a limited quantity. Price, packet, 10 cents, 3 for 25 cents; ½ pint, 15 cents.

POLE OR RUNNING BEANS.

If sent by mail, add 5 cents to price named for half pint, 10 cents for pint, 15 cents for quart, postage.

Fat Horse or Creaseback—The old reliable round pod Georgia Bean. A plump, stringless snap, and good shell bean: bears till frost. Packet, 10 cents; ½ pint, 15 cents; pint, 25 cents; quart, 40 cents.

Improved Southern Prolific—Quick to mature; pods in clusters; brittle and tender. Papers, 2 for 5 cents; ½ pint, 15 cents pint, 20 cents; quart, 35 cents.

Lazy Wife—Very prolific; pods four to six inches long, and borne in large clusters; stringless, tender and rich. As a snap or shelled bean, it is one of the best of the Poles. Packet, 10 cents; ½ pint, 15 cents; pint, 20 cents; quart, 35 cents.

Corn Field or Cut Short—The old popular kind for planting among corn. Very prolific. Packet, 10 cents; ½ pint, 15 cents; pint, 20 cents; quart, 35 cents.

TRUCK FARMERS.

Send us a list of your wants, specifying varieties and quantities and we will be pleased to name special prices on our high quality seed. We are making it to the interest of the truck and other farmers to deal with us.

BEETS.

Soil should be rich and well spaded. Sow at any time from middle of July to November, in drills twelve to eighteen inches apart. Cover about one inch; thin out when a month old. Soak seeds over night. Ounce will sow 50-feet drill; five pounds to an acre.

If by mail, add 5 cents for half pound and 10 cents for one pound, postage.

Early Eclipse—Very rapid grower; smooth, intense blood-red skin and flesh; fine grained and sweet. Packets, 2 for 5 cents; ounce, 10 cents; 4 ounces, 20 cents; pound, 50 cents. Special prices in large quantities.

Extra Early Red Turnip—Of fine quality; very productive. Will make in seven or eight weeks from sowing. Boils red; tender and sweet. Papers, 2 for 5 cents; ounce, 10 cents; 4 ounces, 20 cents; pound, 50 cents.

Edmund's Dark Blood Turnip—Little later than above, but of superior quality. Packets, 2 for 5 cents; ounce, 10 cents; 4 ounces, 20 cents; pound, 50 cents.

EARLY ECLIPSE BEETS. *Crosby's Improved Egyptian*—A choice form of the Egyptian and consequently is very desirable. Thicker in body than the Egyptian; small

necked and dark fleshed. Fine for early market. Packets, 5 cents; ounce, 10 cents; 4 ounces, 25 cents; pound, 60 cents.

Extra Early Lentz—Of perfect turnip form; smooth roots; dark blood flesh; tender and sweet at all times and very productive. Packets, 2 for 5 cents; ounce, 10 cents; 4 ounces, 25 cents; pound, 60 cents.

Improved Long Blood—Very rich; flesh dark red; much esteemed for table in winter. Packets, 2 for 5 cents; ounce, 10 cents; 4 ounces, 25 cents; pound, 50 cents.

Half Long Blood—Follows the Red Turnip in maturity; dark blood-red; excellent for winter. Packets, 2 for 5 cents; ounce, 10 cents; 4 ounces, 25 cents; pound, 50 cents.

White Flesh Sugar—Grows large and is sweet. Packets, 2 for 5 cents; ounce, 10 cents; 4 ounces, 15 cents; pound, 40 cents.

---

60 PAPERS FOR $1.00 We will send by mail or express prepaid for $1.00, any sixty papers seed priced in this Catalogue at 2 for 5 cents.

MANGEL WURZELS.

The value of the Mangel Wurzels and Sugar Beets for feeding cattle, sheep and swine, especially in winter months, cannot be too highly estimated. By their use stock will improve in health and condition. Cultivation is simple, yield enormous and cost trifling. To save them for winter use, bank carefully in a dry situation, as you would potatoes. They should be sliced before feeding; mix well with a little bran, and if possible, steam them. For deep soil the long varieties are best. Globes for sandy soil. Sow in rows two feet apart, thin to twelve to fifteen inches in row. Manure well. Five pounds seed will sow an acre. June, July and August are good months for sowing.

Golden Globe Mangel—Very large; excellent feeding qualities.

Golden Tankard Mangel—Half long; large, bright yellow and sweet.

Mammoth Long Red Mangel—One of the largest and best.

White French Sugar Beet—Grows large and very sweet.

GOLDEN TANKARD MANGEL WURZEL.

Price, any of above, ounce, 10 cents; 4 ounces, 15 cents; 8 ounces, 30 cents; pound, 50 cents, postpaid.

We would be pleased to make special prices to those wishing Beets, Cabbage, Turnip or other seeds in large quantities. In writing kindly state amount desired.

CABBAGE PLANTS.

Raised in Open Air and from our high quality seed. We will ship direct from a long experienced grower, by express, the following varieties, *in lots not less than 1,000 at $1.50 per 1,000; $1.25 per 1,000 in 5,000 lots; $1.00 per 1,000 in 10,000 lots and over:* Our Augusta Early Trucker, Danish Ballhead, Green Glazed and Short Stem Flat Dutch. It is not always best to hold us strictly to certain varieties, but mention when ordering the ones you would prefer; this might save delay.

...Alexander's Reliable Cabbage Seed ...

CABBAGE.

This is one of the most important of all the garden crops, and one which always receives our most critical attention. Upon the quality of the seed planted; the source from which obtained; its adaptability to our Southern sections, largely depends the success of the crop. The reputation we have made for selling the very best and highest grade seeds,

CULTURE—The soil should be deep, rich and heavily manured. For main crop, sow thinly in beds from February to November. August is a good month to sow for a Winter crop. Keep the plants well watered. In transplanting, set the plants in the ground up to the first leaf no matter how long stems may be. Set in rows two feet apart and eighteen inches in row. Constant cultivation of the growing crop is essential to success. One ounce of seed will produce about 3,000 plants. Six ounces will make enough plants for an acre.

Augusta Early Trucker Cabbage.

We claim that this is the best large early Flat Head Cabbage in existence, a variety which will not only give the most satisfactory results in "home gardens," but will prove of greatest value to the market gardeners of South Carolina, Georgia, Florida and Southern States. It suits all seasons; in fact, no cabbage grown approaches it in so many desirable qualities. Sown in the Spring, it makes the best Summer crop. Sown in late Summer months, it makes a most reliable Winter cabbage, which will keep through severest cold. Your attention is called to an unsolicited testimonial of one of the largest cabbage growers in the South. Price, packet, 10 cents: ounce, 35 cents; 4 ounces, $1.00; 8 ounces, $1.75; pound, $3.50.

Improved Sure Head—(Stock from the originator.) Remarkable for its certainty to head. Produces very large, flattened heads, weighing from ten to fifteen pounds; very uniform and firm; a favorite everywhere. Packets, 10 cents, 3 for 25 cents; ounce, 25 cents; 6 ounces, $1.00; pound, $2.50.

Early Jersey Wakefield—Select stock. Market gardeners consider this the best early cabbage, and from our experience we think it fully entitled to its great popularity. *The strain of seed sold by us is the best to be had.* Heads conical and large for so early a cabbage; hard and solid. Papers, 2 for 5 cents; ounce, 25 cents; 4 ounces, 75 cents; pound, price on application.

AUGUSTA "EARLY TRUCKER" CABBAGE.

comes from the fact that we always offer only such seeds *as are raised for us by one of the best Cabbage Growers in the United States,* and such as we confidently believe can be depended on to produce large, solid heads of the very best quality. Those who have become our patrons for Cabbage Seeds, order from us year after year.

We caution our friends against cheap imported seeds—GET THE BEST.

The shortage of the American grown Cabbage crop last year will make reliable Cabbage Seed a little higher, but the best are the cheapest.

EARLY JERSEY WAKEFIELD CABBAGE.

Early Charleston Wakefield—A few days later than the Early Jersey; heads larger and stands longer. Papers, 2 for 5 cents; ounce, 30 cents; 4 ounces, 85 cents; pound, price on application.

CABBAGE—Continued.

IMPROVED LATE FLAT DUTCH CABBAGE.

CABBAGE—Continued.

Danish Ball-Head — (Seed from Denmark). This variety is a true shipper; grows very close and firm; white and of excellent quality; the best keeper of all Winter sorts. For planting at the end of Spring,

DANISH BALL-HEAD CABBAGE.

this variety has few equals, as it is remarkably hardy and thrives even on thin soil and upon a high exposed situation. Packet, 10 cents; ounce, 25 cents; 4 ounces, 75 cents; pound, $2.25.

Improved World Beater (or Autumn King)—(Stock from the Originator.) It produces more *uniformly large heads*—hard and solid—than any cabbage known. Sure to head and solid as a rock; fine grained and tender; stalk short. Packets, 10 cents, 3 for 25 cents; ounce, 25 cents; 4 ounces, 75 cents; 6 ounces, $1.00; pound, $2.50.

Buncombe (N. C.) Winter—The genuine seed, grown for us especially by an experienced grower in the mountains of North Carolina. Large, firm heads, very hardy; a good keeper; reliable to make solid heads when it is properly treated. For Winter use, sow from March to June; for Spring heads, sow in July, August or September. Packets, 10 cents, 3 for 25 cents; ounce, 25 cents; 4 ounces, 75 cents; pound, $2.50.

IMPROVED LATE DRUMHEAD CABBAGE.

Extra Early Market—This is the earliest variety of all; the pioneer of early cabbages; the heads are of medium size and oblong. Packet, 10 cents; ounce, 25 cents; 4 ounces, 75 cents; 8 ounces, $1.25; pound, $2.00.

Early Large York—Earlier than the two following varieties, but smaller heads. Packets, 2 for 5 cents; ounce, 20 cents; 4 ounces, 60 cents; pound, $1.60.

Early Winningstadt—Very early. Heads of good size and solid. Sure headers. Packets, 2 for 5 cents; ounce, 20 cents; 4 ounces, 60 cents; pound, $1.75.

Improved Early Drumhead—Later than Early Summer, but at least three weeks earlier than the Late Drumhead. Packets, 2 for 5 cents; ounce, 20 cents; 4 ounces, 65 cents; pound, $1.75.

Improved Premium Late Drumhead—Prize stock. Very hardy. Better adapted, we think, than most other kinds for Fall and Winter planting and for Spring use. Very large heads, nearly round. Packets, 2 for 5 cents; ounce, 20 cents; 4 ounces, 65 cents; pound, $1.75.

Improved Early Flat Dutch—Very desirable; third early. Two or three weeks earlier than the late variety, which it closely resembles in shape. Packets, 2 for 5 cents; ounce, 20 cents; 4 ounces, 65 cents; pound, $1.75.

Improved Premium Late Flat Dutch—Prize stock. One of the most popular of all kinds sold. Grows to very large size; solid, flat heads, often weigh-

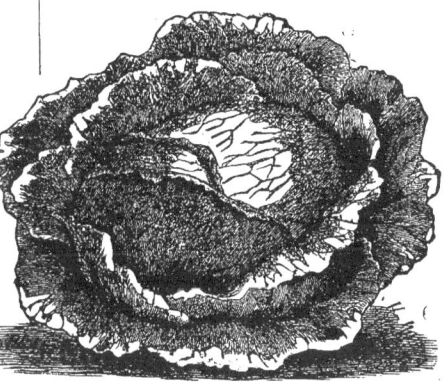

BUNCOMBE (NORTH CAROLINA) WINTER CABBAGE.

ing twenty pounds. Packets, 2 for 5 cents; ounce, 20 cents; 4 ounces, 65 cents; pound, $1.75.

Perfection Drumhead Savoy—Heads are large slightly flattened; foliage dark green with coarse wrinkles; short stalk. The best Savoy in existence. Packets, 2 for 5 cents; ounce, 20 cents; 4 ounces, 75 cents; pound, $2.00.

All Season—Can be planted for either early or late crops. It is a greatly improved strain of Early Flat Dutch. Heads very large, round, solid and of fine quality, keeping as well as Winter sorts. Remarkable for its ability to stand the hot sun and dry weather. Packets, 2 for 5 cents; ounce, 20 cents; 4 ounces, 65 cents; pound, $2.00.

Improved Early Summer—Best second early variety. Heads are very uniform, with few outside leaves. Packets, 2 for 5 cents; ounce, 20 cents; 4 ounces, 75 cents; pound, $2.00.

Fottler's Brunswick—A reliable, popular variety, following Early Summer in maturing. Packets, 2 for 5 cents; ounce, 20 cents; 4 ounces, 65 cents; pound, $2.

CABBAGE—Continued.

Mr. J. L. Dozier, Talbot County, Ga., May 10th, 1900, says: "Gentlemen—The North Carolina Buncombe Cabbage purchased from you capped the climax. I had cabbage in November and December as hard and as fine as any Northern grown. I also had good success with your 'White Georgia Collard' Seeds. If people knew the merit of your seeds as I do, you could not supply the demand."

CABBAGE—Continued.

ALL SEASON CABBAGE.

Green Glazed—(Genuine.) Very generally cultivated in South. Not likely to be attacked by bugs and caterpillars. Packets, 2 for 5 cents; ounce, 20 cents; 4 ounces, 75 cents; pound, $2.00.

Red Dutch—For pickling. Packets, 2 for 5 cents; ounce, 20 cents; 4 ounces, 75 cents; pound, $2.25.

KILL THE CABBAGE WORMS.

Hammond's Slug Shot will kill them and every other worm or bug that destroys Vegetables, Melons, etc. Full directions. Safe to use. Price, 1 pound carton, by mail, including postage, 30 cents; 5-pound package, by express, 35 cents.

CARROTS.

One of the most valuable root crops for the table, as well as for feeding horses and milch cows. Can be sown from July to October. Light, deep sandy loam is the best. One ounce will sow 100-feet drill; four pounds to the acre. The following are the best varieties:

DANVERS HALF-LONG CARROTS.

New Chantenay—Deep scarlet.
Improved Long Orange.
Scarlet Short Horn.
Danvers Half-Long—One of the most productive; roots dark orange color, large medium length, tapering abruptly at the point; very uniform and handsome, sweet and tender. Any of above varieties, packets, 2 for 5 cents; ounce, 10 cents; 4 ounces, 20 cents; pound, 60 cents. If by mail, add 10 cents per pound.

Large White Belgian—The great stock food of Europe. Enormously productive and nutritious; splendid keepers. Packets, 5 cents; ounce, 10 cents; 4 ounces, 20 cents; pound, 40 cents. If by mail, add 10 cents per pound.

SCARR'S FRUIT PRESERVING POWDER.

With this you can preserve Fruit and Vegetables with the natural taste unimpaired. Air tight cans are not essential. Each box preserves twenty pounds fruit. Price, 1 box, 25 cents; 5 boxes, $1.00, by mail, postpaid.

CAULIFLOWER.

Succeeds well, especially in the States bordering on the Gulf. Sow from July to October. Transplant in wet weather to very rich soil and cultivate early and often. Requires plenty of moisture when heads begin to form. One ounce for 3,000 plants. Best varieties are:

SNOWBALL CAULIFLOWER.

Extra Early Snowball—Packet, 15 cents; ¼ ounce, 75 cents; ounce, $2.50.

Extra Early Erfurt—Packets, 2 for 5 cents; ¼ ounce, 60 cents; ounce, $2.00.

Early Paris—Packets, 2 for 5 cents; ¼ ounce, 60 cents; ounce, $2.00.

CELERY.

This delicious vegetable is not cultivated as generally in the South as it should be. It is a successful crop here, and pays handsomely.

CULTURE — For early transplanting, sow in May or June; for later crop, in August or September. Soil should be rich and deep, and plants in rows three feet apart, six to eight inches in row. Plants should be set when about six inches high. Celery requires moisture; keep well watered. Blanch by earthing up when large enough. One ounce will make about 5,000 plants.

Alexander's White Plume—A good kind, requiring but little banking up to blanch. For earliness this is the best. Packets, 2 for 5 cents; ounce, 25 cents; ¼ pound, 65 cents; pound, $2.00.

ALEXANDER'S WHITE PLUME CELERY.

Large White Solid—A solid, crisp variety; the most generally cultivated for market use. Packets, 2 for 5 cents; ounce, 20 cents; ¼ pound, 65 cents; pound, $1.75.

CELERY—Continued.

CELERY—Continued.

Boston Market—A favorite here, and remarkable for its tender, succulent stems and mild flavor. Packets, 2 for 5 cents; ounce, 20 cents; ¼ pound, 65 cents; pound, $1.75.

Golden Self-Blanching—Solid, crisp and brittle; compact in growth; self-blanching to a large extent; is early and grows to a large size. Papers, 2 for 5 cents; ounce, 25 cents; 4 ounces, 75 cents; pound, $2.00.

Pink Plume—(*Henderson's.*) A new variety, crisp and rich in flavor. Packet, 10 cents; 3 for 25 cents; ounce, 30 cents.

New Giant Paschal—Stalk very solid, crisp, tender and of rich flavor. Bleaches easily. This variety is of wonderful keeping qualities, and is comparatively rust proof. Packet, 5 cents; ounce, 25 cents; ¼ pound, 75 cents; pound, $2.00.

CELERIAC.

Turnip Rooted Celery. Produces turnip-shaped roots which may be cooked and sliced and used with vinegar, making a most excellent salad.

Erfurt Giant—Packet, 5 cents; ounce, 25 cents; ¼ pound, 75 cents.

Large Smooth Prague—Packet, 10 cents; ounce, 30 cents; ¼ pound, $1.00.

COLLARDS.

This is peculiarly a Southern vegetable, and is highly prized by the people of this section, where it is used as greens. It is a sure cropper, and yields abundantly. Collards also make an excellent feed for stock.

WHITE GEORGIA COLLARD.

Improved White Georgia—Called Cabbage Collard on account of its close-bunching growth and light green leaves resembling the cabbage—combining the hardiness and reality of the collard with the whiteness and crispness of the cabbage. A great improvement over the old Long Green. You will never know how good a collard can be until you use this seed. Try it. Packet, 10 cents, 3 for 25 cents; ounce, 15 cents; 4 ounces, 40 cents; 8 ounces, 65 cents; pound, $1.

True Long Georgia—The old-fashioned variety; much esteemed, but does not compare with the "White Georgia." Packets, 2 for 5 cents; ounce, 10 cents; 4 ounces, 25 cents.

CORN SALAD.

Makes a delicious salad. Sow in Spring or Autumn in drills one foot apart. One ounce to 60 feet drill.

Broad Leaved—Packets, 2 for 5 cents; ounce, 10 cents; 4 ounces, 30 cents; 8 ounces, 50 cents.

PRICE OF SEEDS IN PACKETS.

Those priced at 2½ cents each are 2 for 5 cents, 25 cents per dozen, or 60 packets for $1.00, assorted kinds if you want them. Those priced in 10 cents packets are 3 for 25 cents; 15 packets for $1.00, postpaid.

GARDEN CORN.

We can supply the *Evergreen Sweet, Country Gentleman Sweet, Mammoth Sugar* and *Adam's Early* for late planting. Half pint, 15 cents; pint, 20 cents; quart, 35 cents, postpaid.

FIELD CORN.

The following varieties are planted with success by many for late crops:

Cocke's White Prolific—(*Southern.*)
Blount's White Prolific—(*Northern.*)
Champion Early Yellow Dent.
Golden Beauty and *Snowflake.*

Price, 1 quart, 15 cents; 4 quarts, 30 cents; peck, 50 cents; bushel, $1.50. One quart by mail, 30 cents, postpaid.

ENDIVE.

One of the best salads. Can be sown from Spring until October. Drill seed and thin to six or eight inches apart. When leaves are full size tie up to blanch. Ounce sows 15 feet drill and will produce about 3,000 plants.

Green Curled—Leaves dark green, broad and curly; tender and crisp in quality; somewhat earlier than other varieties. Packets, 2 for 5 cents; ounce, 20 cents; 4 ounces, 70 cents; pound, $1.75.

KALE, OR BORECOLE.

Makes excellent greens for Winter and Spring use; much more tender and delicate than cabbage. Improved by being touched by frost. Can be sown as late as October. Sow in beds and transplant, as you would Cabbage.

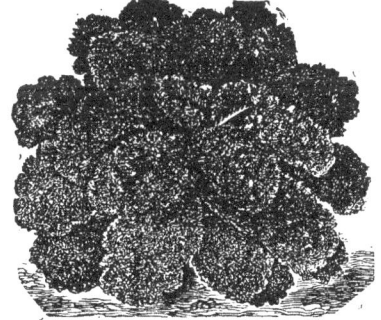

EXTRA CURLED GERMAN KALE.

Dwarf Extra Green Curled Scotch—Is the best variety. Packets, 2 for 5 cents; ounce, 15 cents; 4 ounces, 35 cents; pound, 75 cents.

Mrs. H. C. Stringfellow, Red River County, La., February 27th, 1900, says: "Gentlemen—I bought seed of you last season, and am so delighted that I shall always patronize your house."

LEEK.

Sow in Spring or early Fall, in drills six inches apart; thin to 2 inches. When six or eight inches high, transplant in rows twelve inches apart; put as deep as you can without covering the centre leaves. Can also be sown in the Fall. One ounce seed to 100 feet of drill.

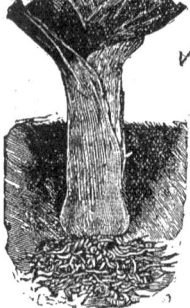

MAMMOTH FLAG.

Mammoth American Flag—A popular sort; very hardy. Packets, 2 for 5 cents; ounce, 20 cents: 4 ounces, 50 cents; pound, $1.60.

LETTUCE.

Can be planted with success nearly every month in the year in the lower Southern States, and in this section as late as October. Plants should be protected in severe weather. Ounce will produce about 2,000 plants.

NOTE—Every particle of Lettuce Seed sent out by us has been thoroughly tested as to germination, and will certainly grow if given proper attention. This seed, however, often mildews from too much damp in the soil, which causes many failures, when it is no fault of the seed.

Denver Market—Large, solid heads; good light green color; slow to seed; leaves beautifully marked; a very fine variety. Packet, 10 cents; ounce, 20 cents; 4 ounces, 60 cents; pound, $2.00. (See cut.)

Improved Royal White Cabbage—Heads large; very showy; leaves broad. Packet, 5 cents; ounce, 20 cents; 4 ounces, 50 cents; pound, $1.50. (See cut.)

---

10 CENTS for packets our Bon Air Ruta Baga, by mail, postpaid. This is the best Ruta Baga ever planted. TRY IT.

Wonderful Lettuce—This is a new variety, and is said to be the largest of all Cabbage Lettuces; very tender and crisp; is one of the best all-round lettuces we have. It will do well if planted most any month. Try it. Packet, 10 cents; ounce, 25 cents; 4 ounces, 75 cents, postpaid.

White Cabbage or Butter—The standard sort. It is early; forms a beautiful, solid head; crisp and tender. Packets, 2 for 5 cents; ounce, 10 cents; 4 ounces, 30 cents; pound, $1.00.

Trianon, or Celery Lettuce—New variety from France. Head long, conical and very large, having a crispness, tenderness and flavor peculiarly its own. When plant matures, tie up to blanch. Packet, 10 cents; ounce, 20 cents; 4 ounces, 50 cents; pound, $1.75.

Henderson's New York—(Genuine Stock.) Large, solid, crisp, tender and excellent flavor; blanches itself. A great favorite here. Packet, 5 cents; ounce, 20 cents; 4 ounces, 50 cents; pound, $1.75.

IMPROVED ROYAL CABBAGE LETTUCE.

Early Hanson—One of the best for heading; large, tender and crisp; stands summer well. Packets, 2 for 5 cents; ounce, 10 cents; ¼ pound, 30 cents; pound, $1.50.

Tennis Ball Lettuce—Favorite for forcing. Makes fine heads and few outer leaves; can be planted close under glass. Hardy and crisp. Packets, 2 for 5 cents; ounce, 10 cents; ¼ pound. 30 cents; pound, $1.50.

NITRATE OF SODA is just the thing to put on Lettuce as a top dressing when the plants are about three inches high. It stimulates the growth and makes the Lettuce crisp and tender. We can furnish this in large or small quantities.

Big Boston Lettuce—Identical shape, size and general appearance of the Boston Market, *but double the size.* Heads well at all seasons. Very crisp and tender. Packet, 10 cents; ounce, 25 cents; 4 ounces, 75 cents; pound, $2.00.

Black Seeded Simpson Lettuce—This variety is said to be of unusual merit for home gardens and the best for market gardeners. Stands the summer heat splendidly. Packets, 2 for 5 cents; 1 ounce, 10 cents; ¼ pound, 40 cents.

EARLY HANSON LETTUCE.

California Cream Butter, or Royal Summer Cabbage Lettuce—A grand, good butter Lettuce. Heads of good size, round and solid; outside medium green, within the leaves are a rich, creamy-yellow color; rich and buttery in taste. Packet, 5 cents; ounce, 15 cents; ¼ pound, 40 cents; pound, $1.25.

MUSHROOM SPAWN.

Mushrooms can be easily and successfully grown to perfection in ordinary cellar, wood shed or barn. We call special attention to the subject, as it is being much discussed in the South, and there are many engaging in its culture, both for pleasure and profit. The Spawn is sold in bricks of about a pound and a quatter each, and directions for planting and culture will be sent with each purchase. One brick is enough for four or five feet.

MUSHROOMS.

English Milltrack Spawn — Per brick, 1¼ pounds, 20 cents; if by mail, 30 cents, postpaid. Ten bricks, $1.50. Special prices in large quantities. Directions for cultivation accompanying each order for Spawn.

"BUG DEATH" kills the Potato Bug, and Bugs, Worms and Insects on Cabbage, Beans, Squash, Watermelon and other crops. Price, pound, 15 cents; 3 pounds, 35 cents; 5 pounds, 50 cents; 12½ pounds, $1.00, not prepaid.

MUSTARD.

Largely grown in the South. Used the same as spinach, or boiled with meat for greens; makes a popular dish. Sow in the Fall, Winter or Spring in rows six inches apart. Sow 1 ounce to eighty feet of drill. The following are the best varieties:

New Chinese—This new and highly esteemed variety has gained much popularity by its extra large leaves and hardiness, also sweetness. Packet, 5 cents; ounce, 10 cents; ¼ pound, 25 cents; ½ pound, 40 cents; pound, 75 cents.

SMALL ORDERS receive the same prompt careful attention as large ones do. Whether in want of a single packet of seed or a large quantity, send us your order.

NEW CHINESE MUSTARD.

Giant Curled Southern or Creole—Very popular in all sections of the South. Papers, 2 for 5 cents; ounce, 10 cents; ¼ pound, 20 cents; pound, 50 cents. /

White or English Mustard.

Brown Mustard—Either of the two last in papers, 2 for 5 cents; ounce, 10 cents; ¼ pound, 15 cents; pound, 40 cents, postpaid.

ONION SEED.

We give the most critical attention to the quality of Onion Seed sold by us. Those buying from us will not have disappointment, either as to germination or definite variety. Soil for onions should be a deep, rich loam. A rich, sandy soil is also good. Large Onions can be made the first year

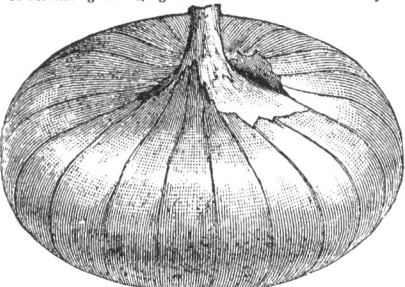

MAMMOTH SILVER KING ONION.

from seed, by sowing the Spanish and Italian varieties in August and September, setting them out when the open season comes on, in rows twelve to eighteen inches apart, four to six inches in drill. Ounce of seed will sow 100 feet drill; five to six pounds to acre. To make sets, forty to fifty pounds to acre. Packets, any variety, 2 for 5 cents.

Spanish and Italian Varieties.

Mammoth Silver King—Very fine. Grows to large size, often weighing two pounds and over: snowy white. Ounce, 20 cents; 4 ounces, 75 cents; pound, $2.

Prize Taker, or Spanish King—This is a beautiful straw-colored Onion, which grows to an immense size. Ounce, 20 cents; 4 ounces, 75 cents; pound, $1.75.

White Bermuda—This Spanish variety is of great popularity in the South. Shape oval; early and of mild flavor. Ounce, 20 cents; 4 ounces, 75 cents; pound, $2.50.

PRIZE TAKER OR SPANISH KING ONION.

Red Bermuda—Similar to above except in color. Ounce, 20 cents; 4 ounces, 75 cents; pound, $2.50.

Australian Brown (*New*)—Highly prized by truckers and home gardeners; very early; much improvement over our Yellow Danvers, Wethersfield or other Red. Packet, 5 cents; ounce, 20 cents; ¼ pound, 50 cents; pound, $1.60. Postage, 10 cents per pound.

ONION SEED—Continued.

ONION SEED—Continued.

Giant White Tripoli—Large beautiful shape, with fine white skin. Ounce, 20 cents; 4 ounces, 70 cents; pound, $2.00.

Giant Red Tripoli—Rich red color, otherwise similar to the white. Ounce, 20 cents; 4 ounces, 70 cents; pound, $2.00.

American Varieties.

Extra Early Bloomsdale White Pearl—(Genuine). Very early; flat shape; delicate pure white. Ounce, 25 cents; 4 ounces, 85 cents; pound, $3.00.

Weathersfield Red—Very productive and keeps well; large size and fine flavor. Ounce, 15 cents; 4 ounces, 40 cents; pound, $1.25.

Yellow Globe Danvers—Is considered the most profitable for market. Early and keeps well. Ounce, 15 cents; 4 ounces, 40 cents, pound, $1.25.

White Silver Skin—More sought for and most desirable for family gardens. Silvery white; delicate flavor. Ounce, 20 cents, 4 ounces, 65 cents; pound, $2.

> We seek your patronage and know that we can please you. Try us.

ONION SETS.

Write us for bushel prices on Onion Sets and Shallots. *Small lots can be sent by mail with safety.* One quart will plant 20-feet drill; five to eight bushels to the acre. Fall planting of Onion Sets are becoming very successful in the South, and should be more largely adopted.

EXTRA EARLY WHITE PEARL ONIONS.

Extra Early Pearl — These we furnish only from September to November. Should not be planted later than November 15th. Quick to mature; at least six weeks before ordinary kinds. Quart, 25 cents; peck, $1.50. If by mail, add 10 cents quart for postage.

White Silver Skin—Quart, 15 cents; 2 quarts, 25 cents; peck, $1.00. If by mail, add 10 cents quart for postage.

> Mr. F. B Wheelis, Little River County, Ark , February 2d, 1900, says: "Gentlemen—Your seeds are the best in the world. No humbug about them; they are true to name."

Yellow Danvers—Quart, 15 cents; 2 quarts, 25 cents; peck, 75 cents. If by mail, add 10 cents quart for postage.

Red Weathersfield—Quart, 15 cents; 2 quarts, 25 cents; peck, 90 cents. If by mail, add 10 cents quart for postage.

Yellow Multiplying Shallots—We can furnish these from August to November. Quart, 10 cents; peck, 75 cents. If by mail, add 10 cents quart for postage.

RAPE, OR GEORGIA SALAD.

Sow tolerably thick in drills as early in the Spring as you can, in rows eighteen inches or two feet apart, in well prepared and rich soil; when six or eight inches high, thin out enough for a "boiling" every day or two, leaving a stand in the rows. When twelve inches high cut off about six inches above the ground and use the tops; when you finish your last row, you may go back and cut again, as it grows very rapidly. It may be sown also to advantage in August and September for Fall Salad Papers, 2 for 5 cents; ounce, 10 cents; ¼ pound, 20 cents; pound, 40 cents.

> Mr. Thos M. Hindman, Winston County, Miss. February 2d, 1900, says: "Gentlemen — I have planted your seeds for years, and am well pleased with them."

PEAS—For Late Crop.

For succession of crops, Peas can be p   every two weeks from January to August. Last crop should be of our *Premier Extra Early* For November and December planting, the Marrowfats do best. Quart will plant 100-feet of drill; two bushels to the acre.

Premier Extra Early.

McLean's Little Gem.

Tom Thumb.

Champion of England.

Carter's Stratagem.

White Marrowfat.

We will mail either variety, except Marrowfat, and they are 5 cents cheaper, postpaid, packets, 2 for 5 cents; ½ pint, 15 cents; pint, 25 cents; quart, 40 cents. Peck and bushel prices on application.

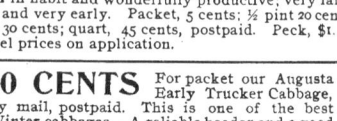

DURBAN'S MARKET GARDEN PEA.

Durban's Market Garden—A wrinkled pea; dwarf in habit and wonderfully productive; very large pods and very early. Packet, 5 cents; ½ pint 20 cents; pint, 30 cents; quart, 45 cents, postpaid. Peck, $1.25. Bushel prices on application.

10 CENTS For packet our Augusta Early Trucker Cabbage, by mail, postpaid. This is one of the best Winter cabbages. A reliable header and a good keeper. Try it.

SEED POTATOES.

We will be glad to correspond with those wanting to plant potatoes for late crop The varieties we offer are especially adapted for this purpose, and should be planted in July or early in August.

"Early Harvest"—A wonderful producer.

Native Bliss Triumph—Very popular.

SALSIFY, Or Oyster Plant.

A delicious vegetable, which ought to be more largely cultivated. When properly prepared is very much in taste and flavor of the oyster. Sow in Fall, not later than the middle of October, in drills ten inches apart, and thin out three to four inches in the row. Soil should be light and deep. Ounce will sow fifty feet of drill.

Mammoth Sandwich Island—(New). Of much larger size than the old kinds, and of superior quality; grows quickly. Packets, 2 for 5 cents; ounce, 15 cents; 4 ounces, 40 cents; pound, $1.25.

> Miss Mary B. Sealey, Robinson County, N. C., January 12th, 1900, says: "Gentlemen—For the last five years I have bought all my seeds from you, and they have proven to be the finest that were sold in this section. I showed my friends what a fine crop of 'Bon Air Ruta Bagas' I had, weighing from two to five pounds."

RADISH.

This is a very popular vegetable. To be tender and crisp, radishes must be grown quickly; quick growth requires rich, mellow soil and reliable seeds. To have a constant supply, a sowing should be made every ten days from early Spring. For first sowing, plant All seasons, Non Plus Ultra, Early Scarlet Turnip, Early French Breakfast, White Vienna, Early Long Scarlet and G lden Globe. For late sowing, sow in August, September or October, All Seasons. Non Plus Ultra. White

ALEXANDER'S ALL SEASONS RADISH.

Strasbury, Black Spanish and Chinese Rose varieties. One ounce will sow fifty feet of drill; five to eight pounds to the acre.

Any of the following varieties, except Non Plus Ultra and All Seasons and Scarlet or Cardinal; in papers, 2 for 5 cents; 25 cents per dozen.

Alexander's All Seasons—This is a new variety; we saw them on the testing grounds last year, and were superior to all others. It is a bright cherry red globe. Its name will indicate that it can be planted and used at any season. Packet, 5 cents; ounce, 10 cents; ¼ pound, 35 cents; ½ pound, 50 cents; pound, 75 cents.

> Mr. R. J. Boyd, Montgomery County, Ga., February 2d, 1900, says: "Gentlemen—Your 'Bon Air Ruta Bagas' are the best I ever ate."

Non Plus Ultra—This is of turnip-shaped and fine round form; bright scarlet color of tender flesh and delicate flavor. Its remarkably quick growth and very short top renders it one of the best for forcing. Eighteen days to maturity. Packet, 10 cents; ounce, 15 cents; ¼ pound, 35 cents; pound, 90 cents.

Early Scarlet Turnip— Small top; quick growth; crisp and mild. Ounce, 10 cents; ¼ pound, 20 cents; pound, 50 cents.

Early Long Scarlet Short Top—A popular variety; short top and brittle. Ounce, 10 cents; ¼ lb., 20 cents; lb., 50 cents

French Breakfast, or Scarlet Olive Shaped—Early and desirable variety, very tender. Ounce, 1 0 cents; ¼ pound, 20 cents; pound, 50 cents.

Long White Vienna, or Ladies Finger — This new Radish is one of the best in cultivation. Beautiful shape, snow white; crisp and of rapid growth. Ounce, 10 cents; ¼ pound, 25 cents; pound, 65 cents.

WHITE VIENNA RADISH.

Improved Chartier—A handsome variety, which grows to a large size without becoming pithy. Ounce, 10 cents; ¼ pound, 25 cents; pound, 65 cents.

Chinese Rose—(*Winter*). Considered the best for Winter; shaped conical and smooth; rose colored. Ounce, 10 cents; ¼ pound, 25 cents; pound, 65 cents.

Black Spanish Round—(*Winter*). This variety stands cold well; grows to a large size and of firm texture. Ounce, 10 cents; ¼ pound, 25 cents; pound, 75 cents.

Golden Globe—(*Fine for Summer*). The best Summer Radish. Flavor mild; keeping long in eating condition; 25 days to maturity. Ounce, 10 cents; ¼ pound, 25 cents; pound, 65 cents.

Scarlet, or Cardinal Globe—One of the earliest of Radishes; tops small, color bright red; very attractive; flavor mild, crisp and tender; is a good market Radish. Packet, 5 cents; ounce, 10 cents; ¼ pound, 25 cents; pound, 65 cents.

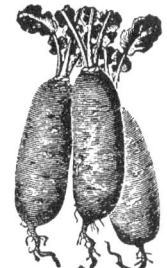

CHINESE ROSE RADISH.

Truckers and Market Gardeners

wishing Cabbage, Peas, Beans, Ruta Bagas, Beets, Carrots, Lettuce, Radish and other seed in quantity, we would be pleased to quote them. In writing for quantity prices, please mention variety of articles wanted with quantity desired.

SPINACH.

A good crop for market gardeners, and finds a ready place in all our gardens. It is more tender and succulent when grown in rich soil. Best sown from September to March. Don't sow in dry, hot weather. Seed requires moisture and cool nights to make them germinate. One ounce will sow 150 feet drill; fifteen to twenty pounds to the acre.

Bloomsdale Savoy — Leaf wrinkled and large. A great favorite. Papers, 2 for 5 cents; ounce, 10 cents; ¼ pound, 20 cents; pound, 40 cents.

BLOOMSDALE SAVOY SPINACH.

Broad Leafed Flanders — A standard variety and largely grown. Papers, 2 for 5 cents; ounce, 10 cents; ¼ pound, 20 cents; pound, 40 cents.

Ever Ready—(*Long Standing*). A new variety of superior quality. A decided acquisition. Papers, 2 for 5 cents; ounce, 10 cents; ¼ pound, 20 cents; pound, 50 cents.

TURNIPS.

We sell only choicest American grown Turnip seed to be had, and will not knowingly offer for sale any other. *Beware of cheap imported seed*, from which only small inferior roots will come. Two ounces will sow 150 feet of drill; two pounds in drills to an acre.

We furnish all varieties (except our *Bon Air Ruta Baga, Extra Early Purple Top, White Milan, Early White, Snow Ball* (*winter*), *and Scarlet Kashmyr* in packets, 2 for 5 cents; 25 cents per dozen, postage included. Two ounces, 10 cents; 4 ounces, 15 cents; 8 ounces, 25 cents; pound, 40 cents. If by mail, add 5 cents for 8 ounces; 10 cents per pound postage.

TURNIPS—Continued.

> Mr. J. T. A. Ballew, Laurens County, S. C., January 27th, 1900, says: "Gentlemen—I have been using your seeds for years, and find them just what you recommended them to be; am well pleased with same. Would advise everybody to buy your seeds."

TURNIPS—Continued.

Extra Early Purple Top Milan—One of the most desirable for early planting. Tops are very small, distinctly strap-leaved, and growing very erect. The roots are small and flat, skin purple on top of the root and white below; flesh clear white; a very shy seeder. Fine for table or market. Packet, 5 cents; 2 ounces, 15 cents; 4 ounces, 20 cents; 8 ounces, 40 cents; pound, 65 cents.

Early White Flat Dutch—Strap-leaved; old favorite kind; medium size; white; quick in growth.

Early Red Top Strap-Leaved—This variety has the form of the White Flat Dutch, but top is purple; grows larger and more desirable.

Red or Purple Top Globe—We recommend this variety very highly. Shaped like the White Globe; of better eating quality; fine for stock.

Pomeranian White Globe—Smooth and perfectly globular in shape; flesh white; grows to a large size.

> Mr. A. T. Hall, Hall County, Ga., April 10, 1900, says: "Gentlemen — I have been using your seeds for nine years, and find them far superior to any I have used."

Mammoth Purple Top Globe — The party from whom we have this variety says of it: "It is the quickest growing, largest and most solid white-fleshed turnip known."

White Norfolk — An old favorite; large and skin white below surface, but sometimes greenish above.

New Extra Early White Milan—In this new sort the extreme earliness, small top and tap root of the Purple Top Milan is united with clear white skin and flesh, making it a very desirable market kind. Packet, 5 cents; two ounces, 15 cents; 4 ounces, 25 cents; 8 ounces, 45 cents; pound, 75 cents.

> We would be pleased to make Special Prices to those wishing Turnips or other Seeds in large quantities. In writing kindly state amount desired.

SCARR'S FRUIT PRESERVING POWDER.

With this you can preserve fruit and vegetables with the natural taste unimpaired. Air tight cans are not essential. Each box preserves 20 pounds fruit. Price, 1 box, 25 cents; 5 boxes, $1.00, by mail, postpaid.

Early White Egg—A very desirable kind; early tender and crisp; in shape resembles an egg.

Early Snowball Turnip—A most beautiful medium sized, round, pure white variety, of excellent flavor. For early sowing this is one of the best; crisp, tender and sweet, maturing in six weeks from time of sowing. Packet, 5 cents; 2 ounces, 15 cents; 4 ounces, 25 cts; 8 ounces, 40 cents; pound, 75 cents.

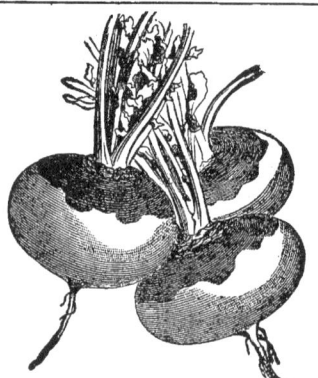

RED OR PURPLE TOP GLOBE TURNIP.

WHITE EGG TURNIP.

Scarlet Kashmyr, or Cardinal—This new and distinct variety is of flat shape, the outside skin being of a deep scarlet color, flesh being a snow white. The leaves are small, full and strap leaved; extra early and of the finest table quality. Packet, 5 cents; 2 ounces, 15 cents; ¼ pound, 25 cents; pound, 75 cents.

> Mr. J. A. H. Welch, Burk County, Texas, January 29th, 1900, says: "Gentlemen—I send for your seeds because they always give better results than any I ever tried."

The Callaway—A Georgia winter variety; grows to a large size; round; white flesh; splendid keeper. Delightful for eating, and one of the best for stock.

TURNIPS—Continued.

> Mr. J. Z. Johnson, Newton County, Ga., January 15th, 1900, says: "Gentlemen—I planted some 'Bon Air Ruta Baga' seed on the 24th of last July and made some turnips weighing 6¼ pounds. The whole lot averaged over 5 pounds. There will be quite a demand for your 'Bon Air' seed this Summer."

TURNIPS—Continued.

CALLAWAY OR GEORGIA WINTER TURNIP.

Cow Horn—Long white; flesh white, fine grained and sweet; one of the best for cooking; also highly recommended for stock.

Mr. D. M. Piercy, Freestone County, Texas, June 8th, 1900 says: "Gentlemen—Turnip Seed purchased from you last year proved far superior to that of other houses. I grew 'Mammoth Purple Top Turnip' to average five pounds "

Southern Seven Top—For greens; old well known kind; stands severest Winters and heads out beautifully in early Spring. *Georgia* raised seed.

Sweet German or Rock—Flesh white, solid and well flavored; a good Winter keeper.

When ordering kindly send us the names of such of your neighbors who plant seeds, and would like to have our catalogue.

Yellow Varieties.

Purple Top Aberdeen—Roundish in shape, purple on top and deep yellow below.

Amber Globe—A well-formed, productive variety.

Yellow Globe—Color pale yellow; green top.

Golden Ball—This is the most delicate and sweetest yellow fleshed turnip.

Nitrate of Soda

Improves the growth of Turnips. We can supply in any quantity. Write for prices.

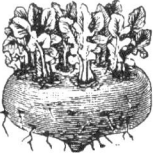

SOUTHERN SEVEN TOP TURNIP

SPECIAL SUMMER OFFER, 1900.—The 4 for 25 cents. We will send by mail, postpaid, a ten cent packet each, Early Snow Ball Turnip, Georgia Collard ,Bon Air Ruta Baga and Augusta Early Trucker Cabbage for 25 cents.

RUTA BAGAS, OR SWEDES.

Our Improved Bon Air Ruta Baga has become very popular in every part of the South. A very distinctive variety, which combines the useful qualities of the old kinds, and, in addition, is so much better for the Winter table that there is no comparison. It is a purple top, flesh of a light yellow, fine grained and solid. Early to mature, and grows to a large size. We want our patrons to try this splendid variety upon our recommendation. *We unquestionably pronounce it the best Ruta Baga for table and stock in existence.* Read what others say about this fine Ruta Baga. Packet, 10 cents; 2 ounces, 15 cents; 4 ounces, 20 cents; 8 ounces, 35 cents; pound, 60 cents. If by mail add 5 cents for ½ pound, 10 cents per pound, for postage.

OUR IMPROVED "BON AIR' RUTA BAGA.

Improved Purple Top Ruta Baga—Very choice stock; the same strain as sold by us for years, which has always given satisfaction. We cannot recommend this seed too highly.

White Ruta Baga, or Russian—While not as popular as the above, it is preferred by some on account of its mild, sweet, table qualities.

Our $1.00 SUMMER SEED COLLECTION...

1 qt. Extra Early Pearl Onion Sets.
1 pkt. Augusta Trucker Cabbage.
2 ozs. Bon Air Ruta Bagas.
2 ozs. Mammoth Purple Top Turnip.
1 oz. our Eclipse Beets.
1 oz. Alexander's All Seasons Radish.
1 pt. Durban's Market Garden Peas.
1 pkt. Lazy Wife Pole Snap Beans.
½ pt. Extra Early Refugee Beans.

The above collection will make a neat kitchen garden. Worth $1.40; sent *prepaid, for $1.00.*

ROFFEA—For tying up plants, celery, lettuce and bunching asparagus; a very serviceable article. Pound, 25 cents; 5 pounds and over, at 22 cents per pound. Write for prices in large quantity.

Mr. P. J. Sharky, Richmond County, Ga., April 26th, 1900, says: "Gentlemen—The 'Bon Air Ruta Baga' Seed that I bought from you produced the largest and sweetest Ruta Baga that was sold on the market. They also stood the Winter excellently. Will double my crop in 'Bon Air's' this year."

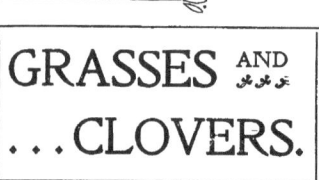

GRASSES AND ...CLOVERS.

Directions for ♪ ♪ Cultivation.

Suggestions as to Selection of Seed, Preparation o f Land and Sowing of Seed.

HAIRY OR SAND VETCH.
(*Vicia Villosa*)

THERE is not a more satisfactory and remunerative crop to the farmer than Grasses and Clovers. Almost any of our lands can be brought up to such a condition as will sustain Grasses, and with subsequent proper care and attention, keep them in paying condition for years. We cannot too strongly urge upon our friends the desirability of adding Grasses and Clovers to their farms. Our conviction is that more and better grasses can be grown here in the South than elsewhere, and that crops for hay and pasturage will pay more bountifully than any other crops that can be planted.

We keep in stock seeds of all the leading varieties of Grasses and Clovers; these are mentioned with special directions for use of each, as herein named. There are other varieties not named, and not kept in stock, that can be gotten as desired; of these we will be glad to correspond, giving all the information in our reach on inquiry from any of our correspondents.

Small lot of Grass Seed for Trial. We have given prices in small quantities so that those wishing to make a trial can order and have sent by mail. Write for peck and bushel prices.

Selection of Seed—Select seed with reference to the purpose in view, whether for hay alone, pasturage alone, or for both hay and pasturage; and also with reference to character of the land. In nearly all cases mixtures of grass seeds or grass and clover seeds, are recommended rather than sowing of any one kind alone. For permanent pastures, several kinds must be mixed to furnish some growth for all seasons of the year. For hay and pasturage, mixtures such as come well together are more profitable than one kind alone.

Seeding Per Acre — Our own observation prompts us to advise heavy seeding here in the South. There is safety and security in a heavy catch, and such as will survive the first summer when thin seeding would be entirely obliterated. The greatest cost in grass culture is the careful preparation and manuring of the land. The additional expense of a liberal seeding rather than a meager one ought not to deter one who is willing to assume the first cost and wait for the results. A fair trial is not made in the South unless the land is well filled with seed to make a close sod from the beginning.

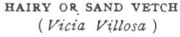

RED CLOVER.

Preparation of Land—Free the land of all stumps, stones, etc., break well and deep; harrow and cross harrow, and roll till free from all clods; broadcast manure freely and plough and harrow it in. Stable and cow-lot manure, phosphate and cotton seed and kainit are appropriate applications. Good implements are important to economical sowing and harvesting. A roller is very valuable both in preparing land and sowing Seed. Most grass seeds are very fine, and bear the least of covering in. The roller alone is better for those than the lightest harrow or brush. It presses them in the fresh soil, which is the best for a good catch.

ORCHARD GRASS.

GRASSES AND CLOVERS—Continued.

Mr. W. A. Pullin, March 31, 1900, Bienville Parish, La., says: "Gentlemen—The seeds I ordered from you last fall are all O. K. I have the finest pasture in this district. My neighbors are perfectly carried away with it."

GRASSES AND CLOVERS—Continued.

BOKHARA CLOVER (Melilotus Alba.)

Time of Sowing—Grasses that grow in the Winter may be sown in the Fall or early Spring. Those which are strictly Summer growers should be sown in Spring, after severe weather is over. Fall sowing is to be preferred for all cases in which it is a proper time, because the young grass is not liable to be choked out by weeds and grasses that are indigenous to our soils. Therefore we strongly advise sowing in the Fall.

WHITE CLOVER.

Although you may be ready to sow in Spring, we believe it a safer course to sow the land in peas and let it lie over, and put the grass seed down in September and October. Lucerne or Alfalfa is the only exception we know to this rule. Sown in February, its growth being upright, it gets ahead of weeds and holds its own very well. Some of the best results we have seen from it were from February seeding in drills. If it is to be put in broadcast, then September and October are better times for it.

☞When ordering kindly send us the names of such of your neighbors who plant seeds, and would like to have our catalogue.

Sowing of Seed—In Fall seeding, it is not uncommon to sow grass with oats or wheat. We do not recommend this, but it is admissible and may be entirely successful if the land is rich enough to give liberal support to both grass and grain. But grain ought to be seeded more thinly than if there were no grass to be sown with it. Sow the grain first and plow or harrow it in, then sow the grass seed and harrow or roll the land.

To get more uniform distribution it is well to sow one-half of the seed one way, and then cross-sow with the other half.

In mixed seeding, as Clover, which weighs 60 pounds per bushel, with Orchard or Red Top Grass, both of which weigh fourteen pounds, it is well to sow the light and heavy seeds separately. In scattering seed with the hand, if some are heavy and some light, the heavy seeds will be thrown much wider than the light. On well prepared soil, surface sowing and rolling is the safest.

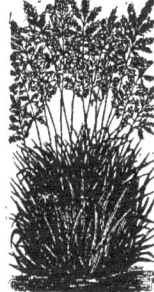

FANCY KENTUCKY BLUE GRASS.

Clover, Lucerne, Johnson, Rescue and others of the larger grasses will bear light harrowing or brushing in. Blue Grass, Red Top and other of the finer seeds are better surface sown, with or without the roller.

HAVE YOU A PASTURE ?
Or, do you wish one ?

If you have a pasture, you can improve it; or if you wish to make one, you can do so by using *Our Special Mixture for Hay and Permanent pasture.* See description and prices on page 19.

Cahoon Seed Sowers Are advised in sowing Grass Seed and Clover. Sows from 4 to 8 acres per hour. Write to us for them.

Prices of Grass Seeds—On account of constant changes in price, we cannot give bushel or quantity prices of these seeds in advance. All applications will be promptly answered, and all orders filled with the best and freshest seeds obtainable.

ANNUAL CRIMSON CLOVER.

California Burr Clover, White Clover, Hairy Vetch, Native Vetch, Schrader's Grass, Georgia Rye, Native Rye, Blue Straw Wheat, Red May Wheat, Fultz and other Wheats, Southern Barley, Native Rust Proof Oats, Texas Rust Proof Oats, Burt Oats, Myer's Prolific Winter Turf Oats, Etc., Etc.

Annual Crimson Clover (*Trifolium Incarnatum*)—Also called Scarlet Clover, Italian Clover, German Clover. This clover will be very scarce and; therefore, a reliable seed will be higher than usual. Reports from different sections of country show that very little Crimson Clover was grown for seed. There will be a great deal of *cheap seed* which will not germinate. We warn our customers against such. We bought our Crimson Clover and tested it, and found the germination of the best. We bought this year the best Crimson Clover offered. We consider this clover of inestimable value as a good Winter and early Spring pasture for all kinds of stock—in addition a crop of from two to three tons of hay can be cut per acre. It is a most nutritious food, and does not sali-

GRASSES AND CLOVERS—Continued

GRASSES AND CLOVERS—Continued.

vate as other Clovers do. It is a great enricher of the soil. It will grow on land so poor that other Clovers would do but little on. The beads are very large and of deep crimson color. Sown between cotton rows in

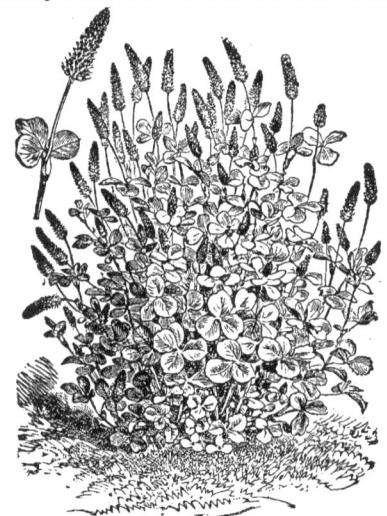

ANNUAL CRIMSON CLOVER.

August or September, Winter pasture is secured and a crop of hay, and ground left in better condition than ever for a crop. In this and more Southern sections it can be planted profitably as late as December, while it does best, especially if wanted for early pasture sown between the middle of August and first of November. It should be cut when in bloom, but before seed forms. Let your land be well prepared and well manured. Sow fifteen to twenty pounds to the acre. Pound, 15 cents; 6 pounds, 75 cents. By mail, pound, 25 cents; 2½ pounds, 50 cents; 5 pounds, $1.00 postpaid. Peck, $1.50. Write for bushel prices.

California Burr Clover (*Medicago Maculata*) —Called California and Hog Clover; a Winter growing variety, furnishing pasturage January to March. It is annual, but re-seeds itself upon the land. Cattle soon learn to like it, and hogs are specially inclined to it. Seed should be sown on the surface of the ground in August to October, two to five bushels per acre, but a less quantity sown will seed the land well for the next year. Stop pasturing it by April 1st, in order that the seed may be matured. The land may be planted in corn or cotton by leaving a space of one foot unbroken between the rows, on which seed enough will mature, and after the Clover dies down the middles may then be broken out. The seed is in a burr and weighs from ten to fifteen pounds to the bushel. Pound. 20 cents; 5 pounds or more at 15 cents pound. By mail, 30 cents; 5 pounds, $1.00, postpaid. Write for prices in large quantity.

Red Clover (*Trifolium Pratense*)—The leading variety of Clover, and is more cultivated for hay pasturage and as enricher of the soil than any other. Best adapted to stiff soils, but does well on any land rich enough to sustain it. It is perennial. Should be cut when in full bloom. It should not be cut more than twice, that seed may mature and drop, thus

keeping up a good stand. No matter how mismanaged clover is a benefit, and whatever else he may do, the farmer who sows clover is making his farm better. Plow up the land in the Fall, and then the corn crop following will make you happy. If you want to make rich farms and make money, grow clover, corn and hogs. It should be sown alone or with grain, in the Fall or Early Spring months, and is frequently used in combination with Orchard and Red Top Grass, as they flower and are ready to cut about the same time. Weighs sixty pounds to the bushel. Fifteen to twenty pounds will seed an acre. Pound, 15 cents. By mail, pound, 25 cents; 4½ pounds, $1.00, postpaid.

White Clover (*Trifolium Repens*)—This is a smaller growth than the Red, and is an essential constituent of every pasture, and all cattle relish it; is of special value in fattening sheep. It is advisable to combine Perennial Rye with other grasses in making a pasture. Largely used in making "Lawn" mixtures, and is highly esteemed as forage for bees. Weighs sixty pounds to the bushel. Plant in Fall or Spring, twelve pounds to the acre. Pound, 25 cents; by mail, 35 cents; 3 pounds, $1.00, postpaid.

Schrader's Grass (*Bromus Unioloides*)— Called *Rescue Grass*; is one of the best Winter grasses; very sweet; makes good hay. Produces abundantly when sown on rich and not too heavy soil. Sown in September it is often ready to cut in February, and may be cut once or twice more before June; or you may pasture it, taking stock away in time to allow seed to mature and re-seed itself. We would advise that this grass be allowed to shed one crop of seed before either cutting or pasturing. Sow in early Fall or Spring, twenty-five or thirty-five pounds to acre. Pound, 25 cents. By mail, pound, 35 cents; 3 pounds, $1.00, postpaid. Write for prices in large quantities.

SCHRADER'S GRASS.

Hairy or Sand Vetch (*Vicia Villosa*)—Is an annual, similar in growth to a very slender and straggling pea vine. Vines often ten to twenty feet in length, and covering the ground to a depth of two feet with a dense mass of foliage. Planted in August, September or October, it should furnish good grazing from January to May; then allow to re-seed itself. Bears the heaviest frosts. Too much cannot be said about this as a valuable crop for hay or pasturage, as the yield is double that of any other hay crop grown under similar circumstances. Hairy Vetch is a feeder of the soil, as it is a nitrogenous plant, and one of the excellent qualities of this Vetch is, it will grow on poorer soil than any other crop, and is easily eradicated, if desired. The universal success which has been attained in the past season with Hairy or Sand Vetch, will make this one of the most popular pasture or hay crops. If you have not tried this valuable crop it will pay you to do so. If you have tried it, double your crop. Weighs sixty pounds to the bushel. Sow one bushel to acre. Pound, 15 cents. By mail, pound, 25 cents; 5 pounds, $1.00, postpaid. Write for peck and bushel prices.

Kidney Vetch—A new and valuable forage plant for dry and sandy situations. It is perennial, and can be sown either in Fall or Spring. It is said to keep green longer than any other crop during droughts. The Spring crop should be with grain as it does not

GRASSES AND CLOVERS—Continued.

GRASSES AND CLOVERS—Continued.

produce a full crop until second season. In appearance it is somewhat similar to Lucerne seed. Seed should be sown at the rate of twenty pounds to acre. The flower is a beautiful pinkish yellow blossom. Give it a trial. Pound, 25 cents; ten pounds and over, 20 cents per pound.

MEADOW FESCUE, OR ENGLISH BLUE GRASS.

Meadow Fescue, or English Blue Grass (*Festuca Pratensis*)-Sometimes called Evergreen or Randall Grass. A valuable perennial grass for a permanent pasture or hay. Weighs twenty-four pounds to the bushel. Sow in Fall or Spring alone or in combination with clover or grasses, one to one and a half bushels to acre. Pound, 20 cents. By mail, pound, 30 cents; 3½ pounds, $1.00, postpaid. Write for peck and bushel prices.

Orchard Grass (*Dactylis Glomerata*)—The best known and most used of the grasses. Its rapid growth makes it popular for pasturage and hay. Succeeds well on all soils (not wet) on open lands, in orchards and open wood lands. Very early and the last to yield to frost. Resists drouth well. Will bear repeated pasturing and mowing more so than any other grass. Sown with Red Clover, they blossom at same time, and it will combine well with other grasses. Weighs fourteen pounds to the bushel. Sow in Spring or Fall, one and a half to two bushels to the acre. Pound, 20 cents. By mail, pound, 30 cents; 3½ pounds, $1.00, postpaid.

JOHNSON GRASS.

Johnson Grass— (*Sorghum Halapense*) — Called also Mean's, Guinea Grass, Green Valley Grass, Cuba Grass. This is a perennial which can be propagated from the roots or seed. Excellent for hay or pasturage. Makes the best growth on rich bottom lands, and will give three cuttings of about two tons each when in good condition. It is difficult to eradicate. It starts early and grows continually till killed by frost. Stands severest droughts; eagerly eaten by all stock, and hogs are fond of the roots. Cut before the seed stalk shoot up Weighs twenty-five pounds to the bushel. Sow in August or September or in Spring, one to one and a half bushels to an acre. We consider liberal seeding best. Pound, 15 cents. By mail, pound, 25 cents; 5 pounds, $1.00, postpaid. Write for bushel prices. Mention quantity desired.

Kentucky Blue Grass (*Poa Pratensis*)—One of the best for a pasture grass. Especially useful in mixtures with other grasses in open woodlands, front yards and ornamental plots. It should be sown with Orchard, Tall Meadow Oat and Clover; stock exceedinly fond of it. It requires rich land; will make nothing on thin soils; low ground, when the soil is dark colored and contains lime, or on seepy hillsides it does well. Sow in Fall or Spring, twenty or thirty pounds to the acre. Weighs fourteen pounds to bushel. Pound, 20 cents. By mail, 30 cents; 4 pounds, $1.00, postpaid. Write for peck and bushel prices.

HUNGARIAN AWNLESS BROME GRASS.

(*Bromus Inermis.*)

A hardy perennial, "standing extremes of heat, cold and drought better than any other of our cultivated grasses." In the South it remains green all Winter. "It grows with wonderful rapidity, and produces heavy hay crops and luxuriant pasture. It will grow well on all kinds of soil, even on yellow sandy, although, of course, on this it does not produce so abundantly, but even under these less favorable conditions it gives a very large yield." All kinds of stock eat it greedily, and the analysis made shows that it is exceedingly rich in flesh-forming ingredients. The seed should be sown early in the Spring or Fall. Sow thirty to forty pounds to the acre. Price, per pound, 25 cents; if by mail, 35 cents; 10 pounds and over, 20 cents per pound; 30 pounds and over, 18 cents per pound, F. O. B., Augusta.

Herds, or Red Top Grass (*Agrotis Vulgaris*)— Thrives on any good soil; is especially suited to low, damp soil; remains in fair condition throughout Winter: not easily killed by overflows, even when covered by water for two or three weeks at a time. Does not make much show during the first season, but becomes more dense with age. Particularly desired for early Spring grazing. In seeding land, it is well to add one bushel of English Perennial Rye Grass, which makes a quick, early growth, and almost wholly disappears after first season, when the Red Top will become stronger and occupy the ground more fully. One of the best grasses to use in stopping washes. Weighs fourteen pounds to the bushel. Sow in Fall or Spring, one and a half bushels to acre. Pound, 12½ cents; by mail, pound, 25 cents; 5 pounds, $1.00, postpaid. Write for bushel prices; state quantity desired.

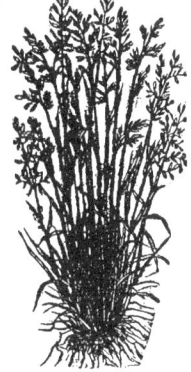

RED TOP GRASS.

LUCERNE, or Alfalfa (*Medicago Sativa*)— This is one of the most valuable Clovers that we have; does not bear much pasturage; gives four to five successive cuttings, beginning early, of valuable hay during the summer. It is best suited to rich sandy lands. Its roots penetrate to a great depth, hence no drouth hurts it. It does well sown broadcast or in drills; take care of it the first summer, after that, with moderate good treatment, it will take care of itself. When once set it will last a lifetime. Cut it as often as you find it grown; do not let it stand to bloom. We cannot recommend this grass too highly to any one who will give it a place on rich lands well prepared. Weighs sixty pounds to the bushel Sow in Fall or Spring, ten to fifteen pounds per acre, in drills, and twenty pounds broadcast. February has proved a very successful season for us here. Pound, 15 cents. By mail, pound, 25 cents; 4 pounds, $1.00, postpaid. Write for peck and bushel prices.

Bokhara Clover (*Melilotus Alba*)—Called also Sweet Clover. Besides being excellent for forage, this Clover is being used a good deal by bee fanciers, as it is rich in honey. Weighs thirty-two pounds to the bushel. Sow in Fall or preferably early Spring, twelve to fifteen pounds to the acre. Pound, 25 cents. By mail, 35 cents; 3 pounds, $1.00, postpaid. Write for peck and bushel prices.

GRASSES AND CLOVERS—Continued.

Mr. A. L. Anderson, Troup County, Ga., May 4th, says: "Gentlemen—The twenty bushels of Johnson Grass seed bought of you gave perfect satisfaction."

GRASSES AND CLOVERS—Continued.

LUCERNE, OR ALFALFA.

Sweet Vernal (*Anthoxanthum Odoratum*)—A perennial grass of sweet odor when cured. Weighs six pounds to bushel. Sow in Fall or Spring, three to four pounds to acre in combination with other grasses. Write for peck and bushel prices.

Alsike Clover (*Trifolium Hybridum*)—Called also Swedish Clover. Succeeds best on moist, strong lands. Weighs sixty pounds to the bushel. Sow in Fall or Spring, twelve to fifteen pounds to acre. By mail, pound, 30 cents; 4 pounds, $1.00, postpaid.

Tall Meadow Oat Grass (*Arrthenaherum Avanaceum*)—Doubly valuable for forage and the excellent Winter grazing it affords. Suited to any good cotton land; it does well on sandy, gravelly soil; can be cut twice a year. To make good hay, cut as soon as in bloom. Much used in combination with other grasses. Weighs eleven pounds to the bushel. Sow two bushels to the acre in Fall or Spring. Pound, 20 cents. By mail, pound, 30 cents; 3½ pounds, $1.00, postpaid.

Italian Rye (*Lolium Italicum*)—Weighs eighteen pounds to the bushel. Sow in Fall or Spring, one and a half to two bushels to acre. Pound, 15 cents. By mail, pound, 25 cents; 4½ pounds, $1.00, postpaid.

Timothy (*Phleum Pratense*)—The standard hay grass in states North of us. Weighs forty-five pounds to the bushel. Sow in Fall or Spring, fifteen to twenty pounds to acre. Pound, 10 cents. By mail, pound, 20 cents; 5 pounds, $1.00, postpaid.

Write for prices on peck and bushel of any Grasses or Clovers, stating quantity desired.

English Perennial Rye (*Lolium Parenne*)—Weighs twenty pounds to the bushel. Sow in Fall or Spring, one to one and a half bushels to the acre, or less in combination. Pound, 15 cents. By mail, pound, 25 cents; 4½ pounds, $1.00, postpaid.

Giant Beggar Weed (*Desmodium Molle*)—Grows in popularity each year. Sow at any time after frost is over, until the middle of June, in drills three feet apart, three to four pounds to the acre, or broadcast, ten to twelve pounds to the acre. Weighs sixty pounds to the bushel. Pound, 35 cents. By mail, pound, 45 cents, postpaid. Write for quantity price.

Japan Clover (*Lespedeza Striata*) — An annual, but perpetuates itself when once set. Makes it appearance early in Spring, and is not ready for grazing before June, but grows rapidly till killed by frost. Eaten greedily by all stock. While it does best on lime soil, it will also do well on red clay hills, where Red Clover will fail. Weighs twenty pounds to the bushel. Sow in Spring, one bushel to the acre. Pound, 25 cents. By mail, pound, 35 cents; 3 pounds, $1.00, postpaid. Write for peck and bushel prices.

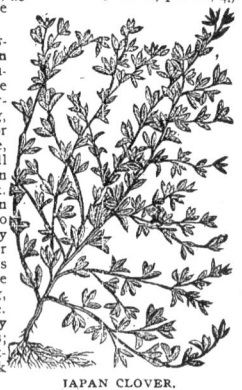

IAPAN CLOVER.

OUR EVERGREEN MIXED LAWN GRASS.

This Lawn Grass seed is a mixture of a number of such grass seeds as have been found to produce in this climate the best results. For the permanency and beauty of the sward it makes, it cannot be surpassed. By its use a rich, green, velvety lawn can be made and maintained with only such care as is necessary to do so.

Preparation of Soil—Have the ground deeply dug, moving all other grass roots. Fertilize liberally

with well rotted stable manure. After a day or two, rake back and forth so as to break all clods of earth, leaving the ground in perfectly smooth and level condition.

Seeding—Plant from September to the middle of November, and in Spring up to April. In our section, thick seeding is always best, and we so advise. For a plot 10x30 feet (300 square feet), use one pound of seed; for an acre, three bushels of 45 pounds should be used. Seed should be evenly sown over the top of

GRASSES AND CLOVERS—Continued.

GRASSES AND CLOVERS—Continued.

the ground and afterwards lightly raked and then rolled; if a roller is not convenient, pat down lightly with back of spade. Take care afterwards that weeds or other grasses do not spring up while grass is young. Lawns should be regularly cut as often as once a week. Use a lawn mower. Water when necessary late in the afternoon, especially during warm, dry spells. After being well established, a top dressing of cotton seed meal or ground bone meal will be of great benefit. These furnished by us are the best to promote the growth of this grass. Weighs fifteen pounds to the bushel. Pound, 30 cents; 4 pounds, $1.00; bushel, $3.00. By mail, 40 cents; 2½ pounds, $1.00, postpaid.

Our Special Mixture for Hay and Permanent Pasture—Variety of grasses and heavy seeding are necessary to establish permanent sods for meadows or pasture lands. We use for all mixtures Red or White Clover, Orchard, Red Top and Tall Meadow Oat Grasses, and add to these such other grasses as seem best adapted to the land to be sown, and the purpose desired, whether for hay only, or for both hay and pasture. We follow the best authorities, Dr. Phares, Prof. Chas. L. Flint and Mr. Howard, in making these mixtures, and have usually succeeded in getting satisfactory results. Two or three bushels are usually sown per acre. Fall sowing is much better than Spring, because there is less interference by the indigenous growth that comes in Spring. Weighs seventeen pounds to the bushel. Pound, 20 cents; By mail, 30 cents; 3½ pounds, $1.00, postpaid. Bushel, $2.50; 10 bushels at $2.25 per bushel.

READ Our directions for cultivating Grasses on page 14. *Remember,* our seeds are of the *highest quality,* therefore, the *cheapest to use.* Use Cahoon's Seed Sowers; we sell them.

Our Special Mixture for Golf and Polo Grounds—This mixture has been tried on Golf ground with much success. Will thrive on most any soil. It was gotten up for sandy lands, therefore has some very hard and heavy grass in the mixture, staying green in the Winter months. Weighs twenty pounds to the bushel. Sow from forty to sixty pounds to the acre. If you have a sandy plot, that other grasses will not grow on, and wish to make a green sward, try our Golf Mixture. Ground Bone Meal is a fine fertilizer for this grass. Price of Golf Mixture, pound, 30 cents; 4 pounds, $1.00; peck, $1.25; bushel, $4.50; 10 bushels or more, $4.00 per bushel.

Cahoon's Patent hand Seed Sower.

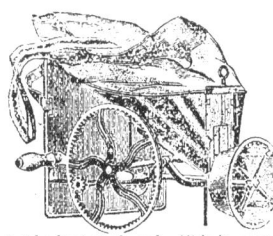

For sowing Wheat, Hemp, Oats, Barley, Rye, Buckwheat, Grass Seeds, Clovers, Millets, etc. The best machine of the kind in the market. The grain is held in a light sheet-iron hopper, surrounded by a bag which will hold a bushel of seed. This is suspended by a strap from the operator's neck, and held in position by a strap around the waist. The seed is thrown from eight to twenty feet on each side of the operator, the heaviest seed being, of course, thrown the greatest distance. Price, $3.50. Directions for using with each machine.

LAWN MOWERS.

Westfield—Neat, strong and durable. Twelve-inch, $3.50; 14-inch, $3.75; 16-inch, $4.25.

Pennsylvania— The prettiest, best and most durable mower made. Twelve-inch, $7.50; 14-inch, $8.00; 16-inch, $10.00.

Pony and Horse Mowers—Prices furnished on application. These are especially recommended for Golf grounds.

"PLANET, JR.," GRASS EDGER.

GRASS EDGER.

Extreme neatness is the great secret of attractiveness in the grounds about a house. The Grass Edger assists wonderfully in producing this effect. It will edge straight or curved work—paths, drives, borders or flower beds. Strawberry growers will find the Grass Edger, with the hoe removed, a rapid and perfect tool for cutting off surplus runners. Price, $6.00.

Araucaria Excelsa (*Norfolk Island Pine*)—This most beautiful of all tender evergreens is becoming more popular every season. As a decorative plant for the house, it is the most graceful and ornamental of all.

Fine Plants, 8 to 10 inches	$1.25
Fine Plants, 12 to 14 inches	1.75
Fine Plants, 15 to 16 inches	2.00
Fine Plants, 18 to 20 inches	3.00
Fine Plants, 20 to 24 inches	4.50

OATS, RYE, WHEAT, BARLEY, Etc.

Blue Stem or Blue Straw Wheat (60 Pounds). This wheat we sold thousands of bushels last Fall. It is spoken of highly by the Experimental Stations. Reports from many of our customers who planted this wheat for the first time last year, say it did well all through the dry season we had. Our own observation of wheat in this country shows that it can be grown here successfully. Many did not fertilize enough, and we had but little rain. Our seed are pure and true to name. We have an experienced man to inspect the crops from which our seeds come. It is as free from cockle and cheat as it is possible to have it. It is poor economy to buy cheap seeds. *Write for our prices.* State quantity desired.

We can can also furnish *Early Red May, Fultz*, and other choice varieties of seed wheats.

Beware! of so called "seed" wheat sold by some grocery and feed stores. Write for our prices; mention variety and quantity desired.

SAVE THE ASHES FROM WOOD

and use them as a fertilizer for your wheat. It has been tried with success. Soak wheat in Blue Stone or Blue Vitriol, two pounds to fifty gallons of water. We furnish Blue Vitriol at 15 cents per pound, 2 pounds for 25 cents.

Barley—Largely used for grazing and green food. Some of our patrons buying seed barley from us last Fall had green food up to May. Our seed is selected and proved to be the best. Write for prices; mention quantity.

Cow Peas—More attention should be given these varieties of field crops; they contain more nutriment as hay than clover. It is the old reliable standby for this section. Weighs sixty pounds to the bushel. Plant from May until August, one to one a half bushels to acre.

Unknown Pea — Called by some the "Boss," and is identical with the pea so extensively advertised as the "Wonderful Pea." One of the best field peas we know of; by far the largest vine maker and producer of seed. Elegant for cooking. Pound, 15 cents; 8 pounds, $1.00, postpaid. We can also furnish Clay, Whippoorwill and Mixed Cow Peas. Write for bushel prices; mention quantity.

BLUE STRAW WHEAT.

Japanese Buckwheat (New). This is the most productive of all varieties, and the most profitable to raise. The grain is double the size of ordinary varieties. Very early; excellent for bees to forage on. Pound, 15 cents; 4 pounds, 35 cents; peck, 60 cents; ¼ bushel, $1.00; bushel, $1.75. By mail, pound, 25 cents; 5 pounds, $1.00, postpaid.

Extra Early Burt, or Ninety Days Oats—A very heavy oats; grows tall and has white seed. This is one of the most popular oats planted in this section. It stood our Winter and yielded more than any oats planted here. This variety can be planted in Fall or Spring. It is very prolific; our stock being bright and heavy. We would suggest ordering early, as there will be a big demand for this popular variety. Write for prices; mention quantity.

> J. S. Barden, Aiken County, S. C., June 9th, 1900, says: "Gentlemen—I planted Blue Stem Wheat bought from you, the result being most satisfactory. Heads range from six to seven inches in length, stalks four feet. I have never planted a variety that has given as good results."

Appler Oats—The Georgia Experimental Station speaks very highly of this variety. It is a rust-proof; hardier than the Texas; later in maturing than the Burt, but earlier than the Native or Texas Rust-Proof. Very prolific. We inspected the growing crop and harvesting; seed bought of us will be clean and true to name. Write for prices.

Native Rust-Proof Oats—Our native grown Rust-Proof Oats are much preferred by many. This is an improved rust-proof Oats. They stand more cold and are heavier than the Texas oats. Our stock is selected, bright and heavy. Write for our prices; mention quantity.

Texas Red Rust-Proof Oats—Well cleaned; stock very fine. Write for prices; mention quantity.

Home Raised Rye—It has been found by careful experiments made here, and by the experience of those who plant year after year, that seed rye raised in this latitude grows much more vigorously and yields more abundantly in grain, than that even grown in the mountain section of North Georgia. Dairymen and stock raisers here use home-grown seed in preference, often at double the price of Tennessee and Illinois Rye. We command a limited quantity of home-raised seed, grown a few miles south of Augusta. Write for prices; mention quantity.

Georgia Rye—It grows tall, and not like the Western rye that runs on the ground instead of growing upright. Our sales increase every year on this Georgia rye, which is a testimonial of its merits. Write for prices; mention quantity.

RURAL BOOKS.

"HICKS' ALMANAC"—So accurately in the past has Mr. Hicks predicted storms, tornadoes, frost, drouth, etc., that he has gained a national reputation—contains weather forecasts for the year. Price, 30 cents, postpaid.

"999 QUESTIONS AND ANSWERS"—On gardening subjects, 200 pages; a book turned to every day. Paper cover, 60 cents.

"TRUCK FARMING AT THE SOUTH"—A work giving the experience of a successful grower of vegetables for Northern Markets; illustrated. Cloth cover, price, $1.50.

"Wheat Culture"—By Prof. D. S. Curtis, Washington, D.C.; illustrated; paper cover. Price, 50 cents.

"The New Onion Culture"—A book of much value. Paper cover, 50 cents.

RURAL BOOKS—Continued.

Mr. O. B. Golden, Screven County, Ga., February 12th, 1900, says: "Gentlemen—I can always depend upon your seeds being reliable. I never use seed from any other house."

RURAL BOOKS—Continued.

"CELERY FOR PROFIT" — The newer improved method for culture of celery; paper cover. Price, 25 cents.

"THE PEANUT PLANT; ITS CULTURE AND USES"— A practical book. Paper cover, 50 cents.

"SPRAYING CROPS"—Why, when and how. 130 pages; illustrated. Price, 25 cents.

"GARDENING FOR PROFITS"—By Peter Henderson. A standard work on market and family gardening. The book is profusely illustrated; cloth. Price, $2.00.

"ASPARAGUS CULTURE" — The best method employed in England and France. Price, 50 cents.

"*Cabbage, How to Grow Them*"—A practical treatise on cabbage culture; paper cover. Price, 50 cents.

"PRACTICAL FLORICULTURE"—By Peter Henderson. Illustrated beautifully; new and enlarged edition; cloth. $1.50.

"THE BEAUTIFUL FLOWER GARDEN"—An important part of this valuable book is devoted to descriptions of flowers easily procured and grown from seeds, bulbs and cuttings, with bright sketches. Price, 40 cents, postpaid.

"PROFITS IN POULTRY"—Contains experience of a number of practical men; illustrated. Price, $1.00.

"FIVE HUNDRED QUESTIONS AND ANSWERS"—In poultry raising; paper. Price, 25 cents.

"BROOM CORN AND BROOMS"—A treatise on raising broom corn and making brooms on a small or large scale; cloth. Price, 50 cents.

"HEMP CULTURE"—The latest work on this valuable plant. Price, 50 cents.

"PHARE'S BOOK ON GRASS AND FORAGE PLANTS"— An old standard work. By mail, postpaid, 30 cents.

"THE NEW POTATO CULTURE"—By Elbert S. Carmen—from the experiments with potatoes for fifteen years. Price, paper cover, 40 cents.

"TOMATO CULTURE"—Tomato culture in the South; 135 pages; illustrated; paper cover. Price, 35 cents.

"THE YOUNG MARKET GARDENER"—A guide to beginners in market gardening; illustrated; paper cover. Price, 50 cents.

FERTILIZERS.

"*Early Trucker*"—The best for all truck and garden crops. We have had so many inquiries from our patrons for a fertilizer specially made for vegetables, melons, small fruits, etc , that we have arranged with the Georgia Chemical Works, of this city, to put up and furnish to us the "Early Trucker." The ammonia is in such form as will give the crops a quick start and keep them growing. It runs unusually high in potash, a most important plant food for vegetables; and the phosphoric acid is in its most available shape. We can furnish it in bags small enough (fifty pounds) for an ordinary home garden, or in as large quantities as may be wanted. Price, 50 pounds, $1.00; 100 pounds, $1.90; 200 pounds, $3.50; ton, $32.50, delivered in freight depot here.

Ground Bone Meal—Is highly recommended for cabbage, onions, potatoes, asparagus, strawberries, lawn grass, palms, grape vines and other plants. It makes a permanent fertilizer, as the bone is steadily decomposing. Price, 5 pounds, 25 cents; 25 pounds, 75 cents; 50 pounds, $1.25; 100 pounds, $2.00, one sack (200 pounds), $3 50; one ton, $30.00.

Nitrate of Soda—By careful test it is shown that nitrate of soda used on vegetable, potato, cotton, melon and other crops, at the rate of 75 to 150 pounds to the acre, will double the yield. Being very soluble, it is a ready plant food, containing nearly 16 per cent. of nitrogen. We will furnish pamphlets on its use. Fifty pounds, 4 cents per pound; 100 pounds or more, 3½ cents per pound; 400 pounds or more, 3¼ cents per pound. Write for prices in large quantity.

Cotton Seed Meal—One sack (100 pounds), $1.00. Prices on ton or more will be given on application.

Acid Phosphate—With or without potash, can be furnished. Prices given on application. Be sure and mention amount wanted.

Special Wheat-Grower—Standard Grade— One that should be used by all wheat and grain planters. Write to us for prices; mention quantity desired.

Land Plaster—In bags of 200 pounds each, $1.00 per bag. Write for other prices.

Makes Flowers Flourish—Flowers are like people. Their health depends upon their food. It must be *nourishing*, but not too rich to force growth and cause reaction. The one chemically correct flower food for house plants is WALKER'S EXCELSIOR BRAND. It has no odor whatever, and can be used dry or dissolved in water for sprinkling. Use it and your flowers will flourish and their health will last. Small size (feeds 25 plants six months), 25 cents; large size (enough for a year), 50 cents. Sent prepaid anywhere. With each package we send FREE the book, "How to make the Window Garden a Success."

Nitrate of Soda in Cans—For use on flowers. Price, ½ pound, 5 cents; 1 pound 10 cents; postage, 18 cents extra.

INSECTICIDES.

"*Bug-Death*"—A comparatively new insecticide, but one of much merit. It is safe to use. Destroys the potato bug, cabbage worm and bugs, squash and bean bugs and other insects on vegetable and house plants. It is in a powder form, conveniently put up. Price, 1 pound, 15 cents; if by mail, 33 cents; 3 pounds, 35 cents; 5 pounds, 50 cents; 12½ pounds, $1.00.

Slug-Shot—Specially recommended for destroying the cabbage worm, potato bug, tobacco worm and all insects and worms; turnip and beet fly. It is ready for use; only requires to be dusted on the plants while wet with dew; or when applied in evening, plants should be watered over the leaves half an hour before the Slug-Shot is applied. Pound, sprinkle cartoons, 15 cents; if by mail, 30 cents; 5 pound package, 35 cents; 10 pounds, 60 cents; 25 pounds, $1.15.

Whale Oil Soap—Very effective for washing trees and destroying all insects on the bark; it is also an exterminator of insects and lice on plants and shrubbery. It will promptly rid cabbage and other vegetable plants. Pound, 20 cents; 2 pounds, 35 cents; 5 pounds, 50 cents. If by mail, add 16 cents per pound extra for postage.

Permol Copper Soap—The experiments made by U. S. Department of Agriculture have demonstrated that copper is the only sure poison for fungi and their allies. Directions sent with each package. Price, 75 cents per pound; if by mail, add 18 cents.

Permol Kerosene Soap—Guaranteed 25 per cent. of kerosene oil. Directions on each one pound packet. Pound, 35 cents, postpaid.

Pyrethrum Persian Insect Powder—Very destructive to all kinds of insects, such as roaches, ants, fleas and flies. Ounce, 10 cents; ¼ pound, 15 cents; ½ pound, 25 cents; pound, 50 cents. If by mail, 16 cents extra for postage.

Lemon Oil Insecticide—The very best remedy for house plants, palms, etc., effectually destroying green fly, red spider, scale, mildew, etc. It has no bad odor, is easy to handle, being soluble in water, and can be applied to plants of most delicate foliage without danger. The "Lemon Oil" is a capital wash for dogs; it cures mange. Half pint by mail, 35 cents; pint, 40 cents, by mail, 60 cents; quart, 75 cents; ½ gallon, $1.25; gallon, $2.00.

Powdered White Hellebore—For all insects. Quarter pound, 10 cents; ½ pound, 20 cents; 1 pound, 35 cents. If by mail, 18 cents per pound extra for postage.

Paris Green—Has been used effectually for the webb worm and other insects. Quarter pound, 10 cents; ½ pound, 15 cents; pound, 25 cents. If by mail, add 5 cents; ¼ pound, 10 cents; ½ pound, 16 cents. Write for prices in quantity; mention quantity.

London Purple—Very poisonous and equally as efficacious as Paris Green, and more soluble in water. Pound, 25 cents; 10 pound lots and over, 20 cents per pound. If by mail, add 16 cents per pound for postage.

Sprayers and Powder Distributors.

EXCELSIOR SPRAYER NO. 19.

We list this year the most approved Pumps for spraying fruit trees, and will furnish those interested with printed suggestions on the subject. Following are the best pumps:

Excelsior Sprayer, No. 19 (See cut). This is the best and most substantial cheap pump sold. Cylinder and all working parts are brass. Throws a constant and continuous spray. Price, complete, $4.50.

Excelsior Knapsack Sprayer No. 1—To be carried on the back, knapsack fashion. Reservoir holds about five gallons. The celebrated Vermoral Nozzle with each machine. Price, complete, $12.00.

Plant Sprinklers—For sprinkling plants and flowers in house or garden. We can furnish either with straight neck or bent, like cut. Price of either, 10 ounce, $1.00; 4 ounce, 50 cents, postpaid.

Jumbo Powder Guns—25 cents; by mail, 30 cents.

No. 9 Powder Bellows—With powder holder, 50 cents.

No. 14 Powder Bellows—With powder holder, 75 cents.

No. 16 Powder Bellows—With powder holder, $1.00.

Cyclone Spray Pump—Large tank and double-seamed heads; tube stationary; cylinder 13x4x18 inches, all tin; throws a spray as fine as a mist; uses about one-tenth the liquid. Price, 75 cents.

Cahoon Seed Sower.

Saves time, money, and sows the best way. We sell them. Write to us about them.

PLANT SPRINKLER.

Perfection Shaker—For applying Bug Death and other powders to potato vines. Price, 65 cents.

Rubber Atomizer—For applying Bug Death and other powders to cucumbers, squash and other small vines, house plants and poultry. Price, 75 cents.

MISCELLANEOUS.

EXCELSIOR WEEDER.

Price, 10 cents; by mail, 15 cents.

PRUNING SHEARS—Steel Blade.

Price, 50 cents; by mail, 65 cents.

STEEL TROWEL.

Long, deep scoop. Price, 10 cents; by mail, 20 cents.

FLOWER POTS.

2-inch .... 20 cents per dozen.
4-inch ...3 for 10 cents, 35 cents per dozen.
5-inch ....5 cents each, 50 cents per dozen.
6-inch ... 10 cents each, 65 cents per dozen.
8-inch ...... 15 cents each, $1.25 per dozen.
10-inch .....25 cents each, $2.25 per dozen.

SAUCERS.

5-inch .. 3 for 10 cents, 35 cents per dozen.
6-inch ....5 cents each, 50 cents per dozen.
8-inch .. 10 cents each, 75 cents per dozen.

WATERING POTS.

2 quarts, Tin .... 15 cents.
4 quarts, " .... 20 cents.
6 quarts, " .... 30 cents.
8 quarts, " .... 50 cents.

IRON WATERING POTS.

Iron band at bottom to protect from ground.

8 quarts, green painted $1.85
10 quarts, green painted 2.10

GALVANIZED POTS.

4 quarts.. 35 cents.
8 quarts.. 75 cents

"Out O' Sight" Mole Traps — Simplest and best made. Directions furnished with each trap. $1.00 each; by mail or express, paid, $1.25.

"Out O' Sight" Mouse Traps—10 cents; by mail, 12 cents.

"OUT O' SIGHT" RAT TRAP.

"Out O' Sight" Rat Traps—25 cents; by mail, 33 cents.

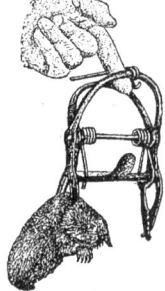

MOLE TRAP.

Stock, Poultry and Bird Foods.

Excelsior Stock Food—A nutritive and restorative tonic for horses, cattle, sheep and swine. Large trial package, 50 cents, you paying express charges.

Egg-O—A poultry regulator and egg producer. Best food for all varieties of poultry, laying fowls, chicks, ducks and geese. Large trial package, 25 cents; 10 pound bag, $1.00, you paying express charges.

Pratt's Stock Powder—Cures and prevents hog cholera. Dairy cows fed on it give more milk and butter. A horse fed on it has its bowels, blood and digestive organs regulated. 7 pound package, 50 cents; 12 pound bag, 75 cents.

Magic Food for Poultry—An excellent food and egg producer. A safe vegetable tonic. 2¼ pound package, 25 cents, at your expense.

Pratt's Poultry Food—This egg producer is too well known to make any comment on same. Package, 26 ounces, 25 cents; package, 5 pounds, 60 cents, at your expense.

Dodge's Four C's—One of the best preparations for chicken cholera; certain cure. Package, 25 cents; by mail, 30 cents.

Magic Food for Stock—A vegetable tonic and appetizer for all stock, improving their general health, keeping them in good condition. 2¼ pound package, 25 cents; 10 pound bag, 75 cents.

Alexander's Improved Prepared Chicken Food—Contains in the right proportion ground oyster shells, cracked corn, wheat and sunflower seed. Price, a 50-pound bag, 75 cents.

Magic Lice Killer—Package, 15 ounces, 25 cents; by mail, 40 cents.

Woodward's Medicated Nest Eggs—Five cents each; 50 cents per dozen.

Zucker's Medical Eggs—10 cents; each $1.00 per dozen.

Canary Bird Seed—*Mixed, pound boxes.* Having a piece of cuttle fish and hemp seed in an envelope and not mixed. Package, 10 cents; by mail, 20 cents.

Mocking Bird Food—*In bottles.* Bottle, 25 cents. *Cannot be sent by mail.*

Ruha's Mocking Bird Food—*In cans.* Can, 35 cents; by mail, 53 cents.

Bishop's Parrot Food—Box, 20 cents; by mail, 30 cents.

Bird Manna—Makes birds sing. Package, 15 cents; by mail, 17 cents

Bird Bitters—A tonic for birds; a health restorer. Package, 25 cents; by mail, 35 cents.

Silver Bird Sand—1¼ pound packages, 5 cents; by mail, 30 cents.

Cuttle Fish Bone—For birds. 5 cents a piece; 10 cents per ounce.

Plain Canary Seed—Best Sicily. Pound, 10 cents; by mail, 18 cents.

Hemp Seed—For parrots and other birds. Pound, 10 cents; by mail, 18 cents.

Sunflower Seed—For chickens and parrots. Pound, 10 cents; by mail, 18 cents.

Fish Food—For gold and silver fish. Box, 10 cents; by mail, 15 cents.

CHICKEN FOUNTS.

Stoneware. Keeps water cool; keeps dirt out of it, and what all chicken raisers should have.

PRICES.

1 pint .... 20 cents
1 quart .... 30 cents
2 quart .... 45 cents
1 gallon .... 60 cents
2 gallon .... 85 cents

CHICKEN FOUNTS.

BOSTROM'S IMPROVED FARM LEVEL.

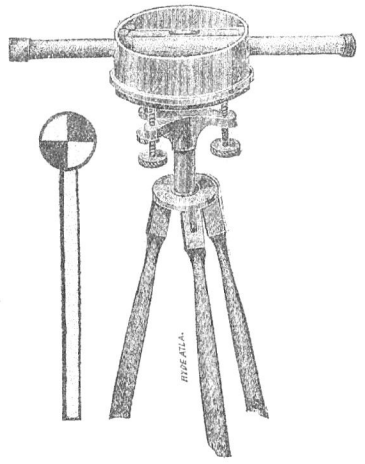

IMPROVED FARM LEVEL.

A treatise of terracing with each level. *A good, practical, up-to-date instrument* that any one can use. *For farm use, for terracing, for ditching, for grading.* This is a machine that all owners of any amount of land should have. Packed up securely and sent by express for $5.00, not prepaid.

STEEL TREE GUARD.

This guard is ornamental, strong, durable and cheap; made of heavy steel rods, galvanized. Wooden boxes breed insects, and are clumsy. This guard is easy to erect and move. Nine inches in diameter, 5 feet, 8 inches high. Price, $1.75 each. Write for dozen price.

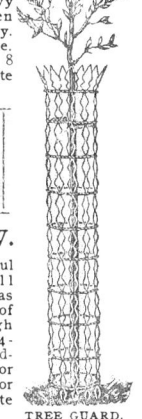

Messrs Hughes Bros., Richmond County, Ga., say: "Gentlemen—The Blue Straw Wheat you sold us last year proved very successful. We did not fertilize at all and the average heighth was about four feet; heads long and plump."

AVERY GARDEN PLOW.

This wonderful garden plow will give pleasure as well as profit out of your garden. High steel wheel (24-inch); handles adjustable for man or boy. *You need one.* Write for *Avery's Garden Plow,* sent complete by us, express paid, for $3.50.

TREE GUARD.

BULBS FOR FALL PLANTING.

We import our Bulbs direct from Holland and France. Roman Hyacinth and Paper White Narcissus arrive about the first of August, other Bulbs, latter part of September. Parties who got Bulbs of us last year had much success with them, and from the inquiries coming in, the prospects are for a large increase in our Bulb business this season, therefore we would advise you to place your order for Bulbs early. Don't wait. Nothing will so beautify your gardens as these gorgeous, sweet scented, early spring flowers.

Choice Dutch Hyacinths.

HYACINTH.

DOUBLE HYACINTH.   SINGLE HYACINTH.

			Each.	Dozen.	100
Double Mixed	Dark Red,	-	5c.	60c.	$4 50
"	" Rose,	-	5c.	60c.	4 50
"	" Pure White,	-	5c.	60c.	4 50
"	" Dark Blue,	-	5c.	60c.	4 50
"	" Light Blue,	-	5c.	60c.	4 50
"	" Purple,	- -	8c.	65c.	4 75
"	" Yellow,	- - 10c.	10c.	70c.	5 00
"	" All colors, mixed,	5c.	60c.	4 50
Single Mixed	Dark Red,	- -	5c.	60c.	4 50
"	" Rose,	- -	5c.	60c.	4 50
"	" Pure White,	-	5c.	60c.	5 50
"	" Dark Blue,	-	5c.	60c.	4 50
"	" Light Blue,	-	5c.	60c.	4 50
"	" Purple,	- -	8c.	65c.	4 75
"	" Yellow, same as double,	10c.	70c.	5 00
"	" Roman White,	5c.	40c.	3 25

If by mail, add 10 cents per dozen for postage.

Cultivating and Forcing Bulbs.

Out-Door Planting—To have bulbs bloom in early Spring they should be planted from latter part of September to first of December, in deep rich soil. Give them a liberal supply of water at first. Just before the very cold weather sets in, cover with a coating of well decomposed manure, which remove early in Spring, and loosen soil around bulb. Top of bulb should be two to four inches below surface of the ground.

Forcing in Pots—Plant in light, rich, sandy soil. If possible use soil composed or equal parts of well rotted cow manure, loam (the top spit of an old, rich pasture) and river sand: leave one-third of the bulb above the soil; water well; plunge pots in loose soil or sand; cover them about six inches. After four or six weeks uncover, put in a warm place and give plenty of air and light. We advise the use of old, well washed pots as being best.

Forcing Hyacinths—For blooming in-doors in glasses, select round and good-shaped bulbs. Keep them in a *cool and dark* place for about four weeks until they have formed roots four or five inches long, and see that the water *always touches* the botton of the bulbs. Then give them plenty of light and sun, and as much air as the weather will permit. Renew water every month.

SINGLE EARLY   SELECTED CROCUS.
TULIPS.

Tulips.

	Each.	Dozen.	100.
Early Single, mixed,	- -	3c.	15c.	$1 00
Early Double,	- - -	3c.	15c.	1 00
Double Duc Van Thol, scarlet,	4c.	20c.	1 25
Double Duc Van Thol, Yellow,	4c.	20c.	1 25
Parrot,	- - - -	4c.	25c.	1 75

If by mail, add 5 cents per dozen for postage.

Crocus.

	Doz.	100
Select, all colors, mixed,	- - -	8c.	60c.
Yellow,	- - - - - -	10c.	75c.
Pure White,	- - - - -	10c.	75c.

If by mail, add 3 cents per dozen for postage.

Narcissus or Daffodils.

There are no hardy plants, that have more points of merit than the Narcissus. Perfectly hardy, growing in most any situation, even under trees. They are much desired for pot culture for Winter flowering. Three or four bulbs can be put in a five-inch pot.

TRUMPET MAJOR NARCISSUS.

	Each.	Dozen.	100.
Alba Plena Odorata, dble. white,	3c.	25c.	$2 00
Incomparable, double yellow,	3c.	25c.	2 00
Orange Phœnix, double orange,	5c.	40c.	2 50
Von Sion (Yellow Daffodil),	5c.	40c.	2 50
Paper White, single,	3c.	20c.	2 00
Pœticus, pure white, red cup,	3c.	20c.	2 00
Polyanthus Narcissus, mixed,	5c.	30c.	2 25
Jonquils, single,	2c.	15c.	1 00

If by mail add 10 cents per dozen for postage.

Trumpet Major—A large and shapely flower of a rich yellow color; an excellent sort for forcing or bedding. Price, 5 cents each; 40 cents per dozen; $2.50 per 100.

CHINESE SACRED LILY.

(Soy Sin Far, Joss Flower, or Flower of the Gods.)

CHINESE SACRED LILY.

The Chinese Sacred Lily (*Narcissus Orientalis*) is the variety grown by Chinamen for decorating their temples or joss-houses on their New Year's Day, which occurs in February. It can be readily brought into bloom by Christmas. It is very easily handled, bears pure white flowers with a lemon or orange cup, and, as it can readily be brought into bloom when in water, it will give a great deal of pleasure for a little outlay of labor. 10 cents each; 3 for 25 cents; 90 cents per dozen. Original baskets of 30 bulbs, $2.00. If wanted by mail, add 5 cents per bulb for postage.

FREESIA.

Refracta Alba No. 1 (See cut)—This is one of the most graceful and beautiful flowers of all the bulbs. Its most delightful fragrance makes it a very popular flower. One pot of five or six bulbs will perfume a house. They force very easy; can be had in bloom by Christmas and continue in succession until June. Price, 3 cents each; 25 cents per dozen; $1.50 per 100.

FREESIA REFRACTA ALBA.

Ixias—These are graceful in growth. The flowers of the most brilliant rich, and varied colors, make pretty borders, or indoor pot plants. *Choice Mixed Colors.* Price, 3 cents each; 15 cents per dozen; $1.25 cents per 100.

Ranunculus (See cut)—These beautiful dwarf flowering bulbs prefer a cool situation, are quite an acquisition to any garden; also make pretty pot plants. Price, 3 cents each; 20 cents per dozen; $1.50 per 100.

Snow Drop—(Zalanthas Nevatis). This charming little flower is the first to herald the coming of Spring. Price, 3 cents each; 20 cents per 100; $1.25 per 100.

Oxalis—(*Fine Mixed.*) Very attractive, profuse blooming plants, pot plants and useful for hanging baskets. Price, 3 cents each; 20 cents per dozen; $1.25 per 100.

RANUNCULUS.

ANEMONE.

This hardy Spring flower is becoming more popular as a garden flower; also used for pot culture. Plant in October or November; or as soon as the ground can be worked in the Spring.

Double Choice Mixed—Price, 3 cents each; 25 cents per dozen; $1.75 per 100.

LILIES.

This is the gem of all flowers from bulbs. Their fragrance and beauty are unequaled. Plant in the Fall, deep.

LILIUM HARRISII (*Easter Lily.*)

LILIES.

	Each.	Doz.
Easter Lily, Bermuda (Lilium Harrisii), first size, good bulb, - - - -	10c.	$1.00
Lilium Candium (Annunciation Lily,)	10c.	1.00
Lilium Auratum (Golden Japan Lily), -	15c.	1.50
Lilium Tegrium (Double Tiger), - -	10c.	1.00
Pure White Calla Lily, - - - -	15c.	1 25
Spotted Leaf Calla Lily, - - - -	15c.	1.25
Lily of the Valley, - - - - pips	5c.	.40

If by mail, add 3 cents each for postage.

ALLIUMS.

This is a bulbous plant very easily cultivated, requires little attention, bringing much returns.

Neapolitanum—Long flower stems, bearing large clusters of beautiful starry white flowers. Price, 3 for 10 cents; 25 cents per dozen; $1.50 per 100.

IMPORTED JAPANESE FERN BALLS.

Something New from Japan.

These fern balls arrive from Japan in January. The roots are twisted and worked together in a ball shape about eight inches in diameter. The fresh young leaves soon sprout out and form a solid mass of ferns, completely covering the ball (see illustration), forming a ball of fern leaves fifteen to eighteen inches in diameter, when fully developed These fern balls do well hanging in a window where not too much sun

JAPANESE FERN BALL.

reaches them. Keep the ball moist by dipping it occasionally in a pail of water or pouring on top. Sent by express at buyer's expense. Price each, 75 cents, or 3 for $2.00; 12 for $7.00. If to be sent by mail, add 12 cents for postage

HYACINTH GLASSES.

Tall, Flat Bottoms, Red, Blue or Yellow—20 cents each; $2.25 per dozen. *All White,* 15 cents each; $1.50 per dozen.

Tye, or Short — Large, round bottom, all colors. 25 cents each; $2.50 per dozen.

Chinese Sacred Lily Bowls (Glass)—For one or two bulbs. 25 cents each.

Japanese Decorated Ware—50 cents each.

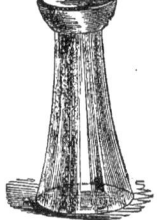

HYACINTH GLASS.

FLOWER SEEDS.

In the list of flower seeds here named, many of them are annuals, and can be sown during the Summer months to advantage. Others are hardy; can and should be planted in the late Summer and early Fall months, needing slight protection during the cold weather. The best results with Sweet Peas can be expected when planted in October and November.

Alyssum (Sweet)—Free flowering and very fragrant. Useful for edging and bedding. White. Packet, 5 cents.

Aster—A flower garden is incomplete without these popular and effective flowers. For late Summer and Fall displays, they have but few equals. Choice mixed. Packets, 5 cents.

Balsam (Ladies' Slipper)—An old favorite; blooms in great profusion. Packet, 5 cents.

Calendula—A showy, free flowering annual. Choice mixture. Packets, 5 cents

Candytuft—A great favorite; culture easy. Makes a showy plant, either in beds or pots. Mixed, packet, 5 cents; pure white, packet, 5 cents.

Carnation—One of the most popular flowers; deliciously fragrant. Colors extremely rich and beautiful. Choice mixture. Packet, 10 cents.

Dianthus (Pinks)—One of the most beautiful for bedding; flowers retain their beauty for a long time. Colors range from pure white to the richest crimson. Double mixed. Packet, 5 cents.

PINKS—DOUBLE
(*Dianthus*.)

Double Daisy—This hardy perennial is unsurpassed for edging shady borders and pot plants. Has been called the poet's favorite. White, packet, 10 cents; mixed, packet, 10 cents.

Hollyhock—Superb double. A well known garden favorite and one of the prettiest Summer flowers we have. Best planted in the early Fall. Choice mixed. Packet, 5 cents.

Mignonette (Sweet)—A well known, showy, fragrant favorite. Packet, 5 cents.

Nasturtium (Tall)—Mixed colors. Packet, 5 cents; ounce, 15 cents; 4 ounces, 40 cents.

Nasturtium (Dwarf)—Mixed colors. Packet, 5 cents; ounce, 15 cents; 4 ounces, 40 cents.

Petunia—Showy and popular plants for fine Summer garden. Fine mixed. Packet, 5 cents.

Phlox-Drummondi—Extra mixed. Choice colors. Packet, 5 cents.

ALYSSUM.

Sweet Pea Offer

For 25 Cents. we will send 6 packets of choice new varieties of Sweet Peas by mail, postpaid.

Poppies—Double mixed. This handsome flower is the best started in the fall. Extremely showy. The brilliant and effective colors have made them popular. Mixed. Packet, 5 cents.

Sweet William—Double mixed. An old favorite. Packet, 5 cents.

Wall Flower—Very fragrant and showy. Should be started in the Fall and set out in the Spring. Fine mixed. Packet, 5 cents.

SWEET PEAS.

There is no flower attracting more attention than this one. Experience has proven that for the best results they should be planted in November. Select a dry situation and sow seed six inches deep in double rows, as you would garden peas, and stick them.

Her Majesty—Large, clear rose pink, an excellent sort. Packet, 5 cents; ounce, 15 cents; 4 ounces, 40 cents.

New Dwarf, or White Cupid — This charming variety only grows 6 to 10 inches high, making a dwarf, compact plant, often spreading over an area of from 10 to 15 inches. Flowers are pure white, two and three to a stem and very sweet. Packet, 5 cents; ounce, 10 cents; 4 ounces, 35 cents.

America — The brightest blood red striped on white grounds. Packet, 5 cents; ounce, 10 cents; 4 ounces, 30 cents.

Aurora—Flaked Orange and Salem on white, large. Packet, 5 cents; ounce, 10 cents; 4 ounces, 30 cents.

SWEET PEAS.

Apple Blossoms—Shaded, pink and rose. Packet, 5 cents.

Boreatton—A dark, deep maroon. Packet, 5 cents.

Emily Henderson.—A new American variety; pure white. Packet, 5 cents.

Orange Prince—Orange and salmon; is quite a favorite. Ounce, 15 cents; 4 ounces, 50 cents.

Primrose Yellow—New. This is a delicate canary yellow, with beautiful shades. Ounce, 15 cents; 4 ounces, 40 cents.

Imperial Blue—A grand invincible blue. Packet, 5 cents.

Violet Queen—New. Violet. One of the prettiest and latest. Ounce, 15 cents; 4 ounces, 40 cents.

Eckford's Delight — White, standard; at first tinted crimson, which becomes very softly diffused. Packet, 5 cents.

We have a mixture of above beautiful tinted Sweet Peas, combined with other choice varieties, that we sell in bulk. Packet, 5 cents; ounce, 10 cents; 4 ounces, 25 cents; 8 ounces, 40 cents; pound, 75 cents, postage extra.

Prices of Flower Seeds in bulk given on application. Mention quantity desired.

Makes Flowers Flourish—Flowers are like people. Their health depends upon their food. It must be *nourishing*, but not too rich to force growth and cause reaction. The only chemically correct flower food for house plants is WALKER'S EXCELSIOR BRAND. It has no odor whatever, and can be used dry or dissolved in water for sprinkling. Use it and your flowers will flourish and their health will last. Small size (feeds 25 plants six months), 25 cents ; large size (enough for a year), 50 cents. Sent prepaid anywhere. With each package we send FREE the book, "How to make the Window Garden a Success."

Nitrate of Soda in Cans—For use on flowers. Price ½ pound, 5 cents ; 1 pound 10 cents ; postage; 18 cents extra.

FLOWER SEEDS—Continued.

FLOWER SEEDS—Continued.

PANSIES.

OUR PREMIUM PANSY.

This is the most popular of all flowers, and it is needless to say anything in praise of such universal favorites. Should be planted from August to November to insure large vigorous plants for early Spring blooming.

Our Premium Pansy Seed—Same strains of imported seeds as have been sold by us for several years, combining a mixture of the best varieties, *which for size, richness in color and markings cannot be excelled.* Flowers from the seed sold by us produce the largest and handsomest blooms ever seen here. Packet, 25 cents; five packets, $1.00.

German Pansy Seed—Flowers very showy. Packet, 5 cents.

Directions for planting Pansies sent on request of each purchaser of 1 packet of our Premium Pansy Seed.

DOUBLE EARLY TULIPS.

..Special Offers..

We make the several offers below, and those made in the Catalogue, as an inducement to those who have never tried our Seeds and Bulbs to try them, and to those who have only tried a few, to plant more of them. "Nothing risked, nothing gained" *Good Gardens and Farms can be made better by planting our Seeds.*

Our Window Garden Bulb Collection No. 1.

The bulbs and seeds named below are the same as offered in our catalogue. This collection is made up with such bulbs and seeds as will give an abundance of blooms, and best suited for house culture.

The Full Collection sent postage or Express paid, for $2.00.

8 Hyacinths—Single and double, colors separate.
4 Tulips—Parrot or Dragon, Petals curiously fringed.
4 Tulips, Duc-Van Thol—The earliest, best for forcing or pot culture.
2 Ixias—Charming plants for pot culture.
1 Packet *Dwarf Nasturtium.*
1 Packet *Tall Nasturtium*—For hanging baskets.
1 Calla Lily—Large bulb.
2 Chinese Sacred Lilies—For growing in water.
6 Hyacinths, Roman White—Quick bloomers.
6 Allium Neapolitanum.
6 Oxalis—Choice varieties, mixed colors.
6 Narcissus—Paper White, quick bloomers.
3 Narcissus (Major Trumpet)—One of the finest.

For $1.00 *WE will send Postage or Express paid the Following Collection No. 2.*

1 packet Our Premium Pansy Seed.
1 packet Double Mixed Daisy Seed.
½ dozen Choice Hyacinths, assorted.
1 dozen Tulips, assorted.
¼ dozen Narcissus, assorted.
1 dozen Crocus, assorted.

For 25 Cents.

6 Packets of our Choice New Varieties of SWEET PEAS. By mail, post paid.

For $1.00 *Our Novel Collection No. 3. By mail or express, prepaid.*

1 Japanese Fern Ball.
1 Chinese Sacred Lily.
2 Freesia's.
1 Ixias.
2 Alliums.
1 package Excelsior Plant Food.

"Planet Jr."

Space will not permit our showing and describing all of the "Planet Jr." tools, but we will send a fully described catalogue, FREE FOR THE ASKING, to any who desire it. You can rely on getting the bottom prices from us on any of the
"Planet Jr." goods.

The "Fire-Fly" Garden Plow.

This tool is most useful in small gardens,
opening furrows for manure or seeds, and covering them quickly. Price, $2.50.

"*Planet Jr.*" *No. 17, Single-Wheel
Hoe, Cultivator and Plow*—This tool is
identical with No. 15, but has only a pair of 6-
inch hoes, a plow, and a set of cultivator teeth,
an outfit sufficient for most garden work. Other
attachments can be added at any time. Price,
$4.75.

"*Planet Jr.*" *No. 16, Single-Wheel
Hoe, Cultivator Rake and Plow*—This is
a very useful one, its attachments are the ones
most needed in ordinary work. Price, $6.00.

"*Planet Jr.*" *No. 15, Single-Wheel
Hoe, Cultivator, Rake and Plow*—This
latest and best single-wheel Hoe, improved for
1900 has a very full set of tools, several of them being of new and special design. A full description furnished
in Planet Jr." Catalogue. Price, $7.25.

"PLANET JR." No. 11

Double Wheel Hoe,
Cultivator, Rake
and Plow.

*Planet Jr., No. 11, Double-Wheel Hoe,
Cultivator, Rake and Plow*—This is the third
year of this splendid tool, and claimed to be the
best tool ever made by them. Its variety of work
is almost incredible. Price, complete, $9.50.
See cut.

"*Planet Jr.*" *No. 12, Double-Wheel Hoe
Cultivator and Plow*—This machine is very
serviceable, has 2 hoes, 4 cultivator teeth, 2 turn
plows. Price, $7.25. This tool is identical with
No. 11 Wheel Hoe, except that it has fewer attachments.

"*Planet Jr.*" *No. 25, Combined Hill and
Drill Seeder and Double-Wheel Hoe*—This
new combined machine is intended for a class of
gardeners who have a large enough acreage in
crops for a double-wheel hoe to be used to good
advantage. It is large enough for field use, for it
holds 2½ quarts, (or about 5 pounds of grain seed),
and has 11¼-inch wheels. Price, $14.00.

Planet Jr. No. 25
Price, $14.00.

"*Planet Jr.*" *No. 3, Market Gardeners Hill
Dropping Seed Drill* — Sows either in hills or
continuous rows. It has a 15-inch wheel, with broad face,
is a very light runner. Price, $11.00.

The"*Planet Jr.*" *No. 5, Hill Dropping Seeder,
New*—This is one of the new tools of last year. See
"Planet Jr." Catalogue. Price, $14.00.

"*Planet Jr.*" *Harrow, Cultivator and Pulverizer*—This tool has rapidly grown into favor with the
farmers, market gardeners and strawberry growers It
has a high frame and chisel shaped teeth, cut an inch
wide each. See cut, for description. See Planet Jr. Catalogue. Price, complete, $10.50.

The "*Planet Jr.*" *No. 2, Seed Drill*—This is a
simple and most accurate Seed Drill, and has been the
standard machine for years. This machine, with the
Double-Wheel Hoe, makes an excellent combination for
large gardeners. Price, $7.75.

"Planet Jr." No. 8

HORSE HOE.
Price, - - $10.50

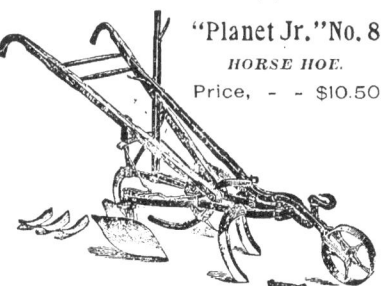

"**PLANET Jr.**"
*Harrow, Cultivator
and Pulverizer.*

Price, plain, - $7 50
Price with wheel, 8 75
Price, complete, 10.50

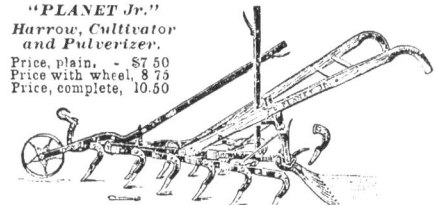

The "*Planet Jr.*" *No. 1, Combined Drill-
Wheel, Hoe Cultivator Rake and Plow*—The
very best machine made for the two purposes,
and does both well. Opens furrows for corn, beans,
and potatoes and covers them. Price, $10 50.

"*Planet Jr.*" *No. 8 Horse Hoe*—This is comparatively a new tool, and has rapidly grown into
favor with farmers, market gardeners and strawberry growers. For full description, see "Planet
Jr." Catalogue. Price, $10.50. (See cut.)

Can furnish this machine without either lever
or wheel, write to us your wants in this line.
Write for "Planet Jr." Catalogue. It is sent free

... *PLEASE USE THIS ORDER SHEET FOR ORDER*

RELIABLE SEEDS, BULBS, IMPLEMENTS, FER

— FROM —

ALEXANDER SEE

905 Broad Street,   **AUGU**

DON'T WRITE IN THIS SPACE.

No...

Rec'd...

Ship'd..

By ....

Checked by...

✦ ✦ SPECIAL 1
FOR 25 CENTS
Early Trucker Cabbage, N
Improved Georgia White (

OUR SUMMER AND FALL (
...... **IS SENT**
If you do not get it, send for it. For every one who plants seeds. It de
Clover, Crimson and other Clovers, Ry **Cabbage, Beans,** and other vegetables a fall sowing. Also **Flower Bulbs** and F in our line.

*Date of this Order*_____*190*   A

Forward by { Mail, Express or Freight }_____ Post

*Your Name*_____ Exp

*Post Office*_____ Ban

*County*_____ Silve

*State*_____ Bills

Express Office {If different from P. O.}_____ Post
2c. sta

Tota

Our Improved Bon Air Ruta Baga.
This is unquestionably the best Ruta Baga for the table and stock ever offered. It is a purple top and yellow flesh, fine grained, solid and early to mature; grows to large size and a good winter keeper. We want our patrons to try this splendid new variety on our recommendation. **Price,** Packet, 10c.; 2 oz. 15c.; ¼ lb. 20c.; ½ lb. 35c.; 1 lb. 60c.; by mail, postpaid.

Liberal Discounts and Allowances on Orders. See Catalogue.
Whether in want of a single paper of Seed, or a large quantity, send us your order.

Quantity	LIST OF ARTICLES WANTED

DURBAN'S EARLY MARKET GARDEN PEA Dwarf in habit and wonderfully productive. Pa
cts.; pint, 15 cts.; quart, 25 cts. By mail, post-paid

Quantity	LIST OF ARTICLES WANTED
	Amount brought forward.

The space below is for remarks about your order, and f
friends who have gardens, are interested in seeds, and who
have our Catalogue. Please give any other necessary correspo

ALEXANDER SEED

*Extra order sheets and return envelopes
will be sent upon application.* }   AL

CPSIA information can be obtained
at www.ICGtesting.com
Printed in the USA
BVHW041337070119
537213BV00013B/236/P

9 781528 019187